FEMINIST THEORY

FEMINIST THEORY
From Margin to Center

Second Edition
South End Press Classics

bell hooks

South End Press
Cambridge, MA

Cover design by Ellen P. Shapiro

Library of Congress Cataloging-in-Publication Data

Hooks, Bell.
Feminist theory : from margin to center / by bell hooks.—2nd ed.
   p. cm. — (South End Press classics ; v. 5)
Includes bibliographical references and index.
ISBN 0-89608-614-3 (cloth) — ISBN 0-89608-613-5 (paper)
1. Feminism—United States—Evaluation. 2. Afro-American women—Attitudes. 3. Marginality, Social—United States. 4. Feminist theory. I. Title. II. Series.
HQ1426 .H675 1999
305.42'0973—dc21   99-053683

South End Press, 7 Brookline Street, #1, Cambridge, MA 02139
         05 04   5

For us sisters—Angela, Gwenda, Valeria, Theresa, Sarah
For all we have shared
For all we have come through together
For continuing closeness

Table of Contents

ACKNOWLEDGMENTS

Not all women, in fact, very few, have had the good fortune to live and work among women and men actively involved in feminist movement. Many of us live in circumstances and environments where we must engage in feminist struggle alone, with only occasional support and affirmation. During much of the writing of *Ain't I a Woman: Black Women and Feminism* I worked in isolation. It was my hope that the publication of this work would draw me closer to feminist activists, especially black women. Ironically, some of the most outspoken black women active in feminist movement responded by trashing both it and me. While I expected serious, rigorous evaluation of my work, I was totally unprepared for the hostility and contempt shown me by women whom I did not and do not see as enemies. Despite their responses I share with them an ongoing commitment to feminist struggle. To me this does not mean that we must approach feminism from the same perspective. It does mean that we have a basis for communication, that our political commitments should lead us to talk and struggle together. Unfortunately it is often easier to ignore, dismiss, reject, and even hurt one another rather than engage in constructive confrontation.

Were it not for the overwhelmingly positive responses to the book from black women who felt it compelled them to either rethink or think for the first time about the impact of sexism on our lives and the importance of feminist movement, I might have become terribly disheartened and disillusioned. Thanks to them and many other women and men, this book was not written in isolation.

I am especially grateful for the care and affirmation given me by Valeria and Gwenda, my younger sisters; Beverly, my friend and comrade; Nate, my companion; and the South End Press collective. Such encouragement renews my commitment to feminist politics and strengthens my conviction that the value of feminist writing must be determined not only by the way a work is received among feminist activists but by the extent to which it draws women and men who are outside feminist struggle inside.

SEEING THE LIGHT
Visionary Feminism

Feminist movement continues to be one of the most powerful struggles for social justice taking place in the world today. I finished the first draft of my first feminist book, *Ain't I a Woman: Black Women and Feminism,* when I was nineteen. It was published almost ten years later. In those ten years I became more and more involved in creating feminist theory. Often when individuals talk or write about contemporary feminist movement they make it seem as though there was a set body of feminist principles and beliefs that served as a foundation from the very beginning. In actuality when feminist uprising began to occur in the late '60s, it manifested itself in diverse settings among women who often had no knowledge of one another's existence. There was no clearly defined platform.

While Betty Friedan was writing about "the problem that has no name," addressing the way sexist discrimination affected highly educated white women with class privilege, Septima Clark, Ella Baker, Fannie Lou Hamer, and Ann Moody, along with individual black women across the nation, were challenging the sexism within black civil rights movement. Appropriating the vernacular of black liberation, white women called their resistance to sexism women's liberation.

We do not know who "first" used the term "women's liberation." That is not important. Significantly what we know from charting the history of contemporary feminist movement is that individual women were rebelling against sexism all over the place. When those women began to meet and talk together, that collective rebellion came to be known as women's liberation and would later evolve into feminist movement. Feminist struggle takes place anytime anywhere any female or male resists sexism, sexist exploitation, and oppression. Feminist movement happens when groups of people come together with an organized strategy to take action to eliminate patriarchy.

I came to feminist consciousness in the patriarchal household of my upbringing. And launched feminist rebellion by choosing higher education against the patriarchal beliefs of my father and the fears of my mother that too much education would leave me "unfit" to be a real woman. I joined feminist movement my sophomore year in college. On campuses everywhere young women engaged in radical politics (black liberation struggle, socialism, anti-war, and environmental rights) were concentrating our attention on gender. Drawing upon the work of the activists who had launched women's liberation, creating manifestos and position papers, female students everywhere were encouraged to examine the past, to find and uncover our hidden stories, our feminist legacies. And while that work was happening, another field of woman-centered scholarship was coming into being—feminist theory.

Unlike the feminist scholarship that was focusing on recovering past history, forgotten heroines, writers, etc., or the work that was about documenting from a social science perspective the current realities of women's lives, initially feminist theory was the site for the critical interrogation and re-imagining of sexist gender roles. It was to provide a revolutionary blueprint for the movement—one that when followed would lead us in the direction of transforming patriarchal culture. By the late '70s feminist thinkers were already engaging in dialectical critique of the feminist thinking that had emerged from late '60s radicalism. That critique formed the basis of re-visionist feminist theory.

Feminist thought and practice were fundamentally altered when radical women of color and white women allies began to rigorously challenge the notion that "gender" was the primary factor determining a woman's fate. I can still recall how it upset everyone in the first women's studies class I attended—a class where everyone except me was white and female and mostly from privileged class backgrounds—when I interrupted a discussion about the origins of domination in which it was argued that when a child is coming out of the womb the factor deemed most important is gender. I stated that when the child of two black parents is coming out of the womb the factor that is considered first is skin color, then gender, because race and gender will determine that child's fate. Looking at the interlocking nature of gender, race, and class was the perspective that changed the direction of feminist thought.

Early on in feminist movement we found that it was easier to accept the reality that gender, race, and class combined determined female destiny, and much more difficult to understand how this should concretely shape and inform feminist practice. While feminists talked often about the necessity of building a mass-based feminist movement, there was no sound foundation on which to structure this movement. The women's liberation movement has not only been structured on a narrow platform, it primarily called attention to issues relevant primarily to women (mostly white) with class privilege. We needed theory mapping thought and strategy for a mass-based movement, theory that would examine our culture from a feminist standpoint rooted in an understanding of gender, race, and class. In response to that need I wrote *Feminist Theory: From Margin to Center*.

Nowadays it has become so commonplace for individuals doing feminist work to evoke gender, race, and class, it is often forgotten that initially most feminist thinkers, many of whom were white and from privileged class backgrounds, were hostile to adopting this perspective. Radical/revolutionary feminist thinkers who wanted to talk about gender from a race-sex-class perspective were accused of being traitors, destroying the movement, shifting the focus. Often our work was ignored or ruthlessly critiqued, deemed not scholarly enough or too polemical. In those days black women/women of color were often encouraged by white comrades to talk about race while our ideas about all other aspects of feminist movement were ignored. We effectively protested this ghettoization of our perspectives, sharing our commitment to creating feminist theory that would address a wide range of feminist concerns. That commitment is the ethical foundation of *Feminist Theory: From Margin to Center*.

One of the most affirming aspects of feminist movement has been the formation of an intellectual environment where there has been sustained dialectal critique and exchange. Hearing the voices of radical thinkers (among them the voices of women of color), the face of feminist theory and practice changed. Many unenlightened white women broke down the wall of denial and began to examine anew how they had talked and written about gender in the past. There has been no other movement for social justice in our society that has been as self-critical as feminist movement. Feminist willingness to change direction when needed has been a major source of strength and vitality in feminist struggle. That internal critique is essential to any politics of transformation. Just as our lives are not fixed or static but always changing, our theory must remain fluid, open, responsive to new information.

When *Feminist Theory: From Margin to Center* was first published, it was welcomed and praised by feminist thinkers who wanted a new vision. Even so, individual readers found the theory offered "provocative," "unsettling." Words like "merciless dissection" were used by reviewers describing the book. At that time mainstream feminists simply ignored this work and any other feminist theory that was perceived as "too critical" or "too radical." As a visionary work *Feminist Theory: From Margin to Center* was presented to a feminist world that was not yet ready for it. Slowly, as more feminist thinkers (particularly white women) accepted looking at gender from the perspective of race, sex, and class, this work began to receive the attention it merited. It took its place among other visionary texts that were altering in a positive and constructive way contemporary feminist thought.

The blueprint for feminist movement presented in *Feminist Theory: From Margin to Center* is amazingly sound. As relevant to our current situation as it was years ago, it offers guidelines on which to build the mass-based feminist movement we still desperately need. Written in a language that is far more accessible than much current feminist theory, it embodies the feminist hope that we can find common languages to spread the word. Since it was first published, feminist scholarship and theory has become far removed from the lives of most people in this society. And it is this distance that makes feminist thinking appear rarified and irrelevant to most people. In the book I emphasize that we need feminist writing that speaks to everyone; that without it feminist education for critical consciousness cannot happen.

Feminist movement has created profound positive changes in the lives of girls and boys, women and men, living in our society, in a political system of imperialist, white supremacist, capitalist patriarchy. And even though trashing feminism has become commonplace, the reality remains: everyone has benefited from the cultural revolutions put in place by contemporary feminist movement. It has changed how we see work, how we work, and how we love. And yet feminist movement has not created sustained feminist revolution. It has not ended patriarchy, eradicating sexism and sexist exploitation and oppression. And as a consequence feminist gains are always at risk.

We are already witnessing powerful losses in the arena of reproductive rights. Violence against females is escalating. The work force is daily re-instating gender biases. Harsh critics of feminism blame family violence on the movement, urging women and men to turn their backs on feminist thinking and return to sexist-defined gender roles. Patriarchal mass media either trashes feminism or tells the public it is an unnecessary, dead movement. Opportunistic women applaud feminist success, then tell us the movement is no longer needed, as "all women have improved their lives" in a world where women are fast becoming the majority of our nation's poor, where single mothers are pathologized, where no state aid is available to help the needy and indigent, where most females of all ages have no access to basic health care. Yet given these dire realities, visionary feminist discourse is increasingly only talked about in the corridors of the educated elite. If it remains there the feminist message will not be heard, and ultimately feminist movement will end.

To begin feminist struggle anew, to ensure that we are moving into feminist futures, we still need feminist theory that speaks to everyone, that lets everyone know that feminist movement can change their lives for the better. This theory, like the analysis offered in *Feminist Theory: From Margin to Center,* will always challenge, shake us up, provoke, shift our paradigms, change the way we think, turn us around. That's what revolution does. And feminist revolution is needed if we are to live in a world without sexism; where peace, freedom, and justice prevail; where there is no domination. If we follow a feminist path, this is where it leads. *Feminist Theory: From Margin to Center* will continue to be a guiding light.

New York City
January 2000

PREFACE TO THE FIRST EDITION

To be in the margin is to be part of the whole but outside the main body. For black Americans living in a small Kentucky town, the railroad tracks were a daily reminder of our marginality. Across those tracks were paved streets, stores we could not enter, restaurants we could not eat in, and people we could not look directly in the face. Across those tracks was a world we could work in as maids, as janitors, as prostitutes, as long as it was in a service capacity. We could enter that world, but we could not live there. We had always to return to the margin, to beyond the tracks, to shacks and abandoned houses on the edge of town.

There were laws to ensure our return. To not return was to risk being punished. Living as we did—on the edge—we developed a particular way of seeing reality. We looked both from the outside in and from the inside out. We focused our attention on the center as well as on the margin. We understood both. This mode of seeing reminded us of the existence of a whole universe, a main body made up of both margin and center. Our survival depended on an ongoing public awareness of the separation between margin and center and an ongoing private acknowledgment that we were a necessary, vital part of that whole.

This sense of wholeness, impressed upon our consciousness by the structure of our daily lives, provided us an oppositional world view—a mode of seeing unknown to most of our oppressors—that sustained us, aided us in our struggle to transcend poverty and despair, strengthened our sense of self and our solidarity.

The willingness to explore all possibilities has characterized my perspective in writing *Feminist Theory: From Margin to Center.* Much feminist theory emerges from privileged women who live at the center, whose perspectives on reality rarely include knowledge and awareness of the lives of women and men who live on the margin. As a consequence, feminist theory lacks wholeness, lacks the broad analysis that could encompass a variety of human experiences. Although feminist theorists are aware of the need to develop ideas and analysis that encompass a larger number of experiences that serve to unify rather than to polarize, such theory is complex and slow in formation. At its most visionary, it will emerge from individuals who have knowledge of both margin and center.

It was the dearth of material by and about black women that led me to begin the research and writing of *Ain't I a Woman: Black Women and Feminism.* It is the absence of feminist theory that addresses margin and center that has led me to write this book. In the pages ahead, I explore the limitations of various aspects of feminist theory and practice, proposing new directions. I try to avoid repeating ideas that are widely known and discussed, concentrating instead on exploring different issues or new perspectives on old issues. As a consequence, some chapters are lengthy and others quite short; none are intended as comprehensive analyses. Throughout the work my thoughts have been shaped by the conviction that feminism must become a mass-based political movement if it is to have a revolutionary, transformative impact on society.

BLACK WOMEN
Shaping Feminist Theory

Feminism in the United States has never emerged from the women who are most victimized by sexist oppression; women who are daily beaten down, mentally, physically, and spiritually—women who are powerless to change their condition in life. They are a silent majority. A mark of their victimization is that they accept their lot in life without visible question, without organized protest, without collective anger or rage. Betty Friedan's *The Feminine Mystique* is still heralded as having paved the way for contemporary feminist movement—it was written as if these women did not exist. (Although *The Feminine Mystique* has been criticized and even attacked from various fronts, I call attention to it again because certain biased premises about the nature of women's social status put forth initially in this text continue to shape the tenor and direction of feminist movement.)

Friedan's famous phrase, "the problem that has no name," often quoted to describe the condition of women in this society, actually referred to the plight of a select group of college-educated, middle- and upper-class, married white women—housewives bored with leisure, with the home, with children, with buying products, who wanted more out of life. Friedan concludes her first chapter by stating: "We can no longer ignore that voice within women that says: 'I want something more than my husband and my children and my house.'" That "more" she defined as careers. She did not discuss who would be called in to take care of the children and maintain the home if more women like herself were freed from their house labor and given equal access with white men to the professions. She did not speak of the needs of women without men, without children, without homes. She ignored the existence of all non-white women and poor white women. She did not tell readers whether it was more fulfilling to be a maid, a babysitter, a factory worker, a clerk, or a prostitute than to be a leisure-class housewife.

She made her plight and the plight of white women like herself synonymous with a condition affecting all American women. In so doing, she deflected attention away from her classism, her racism, her sexist attitudes towards the masses of American women. In the context of her book, Friedan makes clear that the women she saw as victimized by sexism were college-educated white women who were compelled by sexist conditioning to remain in the home. She contends:

> It is urgent to understand how the very condition of being a housewife can create a sense of emptiness, non-existence, nothingness in women. There are aspects of the housewife role that make it almost impossible for a woman of adult intelligence to retain a sense of human identity, the firm core of self or "I" without which a human being, man or woman, is not truly alive. For women of ability in America today, I am convinced that there is something about the housewife state itself that is dangerous.

Specific problems and dilemmas of leisure-class white housewives were real concerns that merited consideration and change, but they were not the pressing political concerns of masses of women. Masses of women were concerned about economic survival, ethnic and racial discrimination, etc. When Friedan wrote *The Feminine Mystique,* more than one-third of all women were in the work force. Although many women longed to be housewives, only women with leisure time and money could actually shape their identities on the model of the feminine mystique. They were women who, in Friedan's words, were "told by the most advanced thinkers of our time to go back and live their lives as if they were Noras, restricted to the doll's house by Victorian prejudices."

From her early writing, it appears that Friedan never wondered whether or not the plight of college-educated white housewives was an adequate reference point by which to gauge the impact of sexism or sexist oppression on the lives of women in American society. Nor did she move beyond her own life experience to acquire an expanded perspective on the lives of women in the United States. I say this not to discredit her work. It remains a useful discussion of the impact of sexist discrimination on a select group of women. Examined from a different perspective, it can also be seen as a case study of narcissism, insensitivity, sentimentality, and self-indulgence, which reaches its peak when Friedan, in a chapter titled "Progressive Dehumanization," makes a comparison between the psychological effects of isolation on white housewives and the impact of confinement on the self-concept of prisoners in Nazi concentration camps.

Friedan was a principal shaper of contemporary feminist thought. Significantly, the one-dimensional perspective on women's reality presented in her book became a marked feature of the contemporary feminist movement. Like Friedan before them, white women who dominate feminist discourse today rarely question whether or not their perspective on women's reality is true to the lived experiences of women as a collective group. Nor are they aware of the extent to which their perspectives reflect race and class biases, although there has been a greater awareness of biases in recent years. Racism abounds in the writings of white feminists, reinforcing white supremacy and negating the possibility that women will bond politically across ethnic and racial boundaries. Past feminist refusal to draw attention to and attack racial hierarchies suppressed the link between race and class. Yet class structure in American society has been shaped by the racial politic of white supremacy; it is only by analyzing racism and its function in capitalist society that a thorough understanding of class relationships can emerge. Class struggle is inextricably bound to the struggle to end racism. Urging women to explore the full implication of class in an early essay, "The Last Straw," Rita Mae Brown explained:

> Class is much more than Marx's definition of relationship to the means of production. Class involves your behavior, your basic assumptions about life. Your experience (determined by your class)

validates those assumptions, how you are taught to behave, what
you expect from yourself and from others, your concept of a future, how you understand problems and solve them, how you
think, feel, act. It is these behavioral patterns that middle-class
women resist recognizing although they may be perfectly willing
to accept class in Marxist terms, a neat trick that helps them avoid
really dealing with class behavior and changing that behavior in
themselves. It is these behavioral patterns which must be recognized, understood, and changed.

White women who dominate feminist discourse, who for the most
part make and articulate feminist theory, have little or no understanding of white supremacy as a racial politic, of the psychological impact
of class, of their political status within a racist, sexist, capitalist state.

It is this lack of awareness that, for example, leads Leah Fritz to
write in *Dreamers and Dealers,* a discussion of the current women's
movement published in 1979:

> Women's suffering under sexist tyranny is a common bond
> among all women, transcending the particulars of the different
> forms that tyranny takes. *Suffering cannot be measured and compared
> quantitatively.* Is the enforced idleness and vacuity of a "rich"
> woman, which leads her to madness and/or suicide, greater or
> less than the suffering of a poor woman who barely survives on
> welfare but retains somehow her spirit? There is no way to mea-
> sure such difference, but should these two women survey each
> other without the screen of patriarchal class, they may find a com-
> monality in the fact that they are both oppressed, both miserable.

Fritz's statement is another example of wishful thinking, as well as
the conscious mystification of social divisions between women that
has characterized much feminist expression. While it is evident that
many women suffer from sexist tyranny, there is little indication that
this forges "a common bond among all women." There is much evi-
dence substantiating the reality that race and class identity creates
differences in quality of life, social status, and lifestyle that take precedence over the common experience women share—differences
that are rarely transcended. The motives of materially privileged, educated white women with a variety of career and lifestyle options

available to them must be questioned when they insist that "suffering cannot be measured." Fritz is by no means the first white feminist to make this statement. It is a statement that I have never heard a poor woman of any race make. Although there is much I would take issue with in Benjamin Barber's critique of the women's movement, *Liberating Feminism,* I agree with his assertion:

> Suffering is not necessarily a fixed and universal experience that can be measured by a single rod: it is related to situations, needs, and aspirations. But there must be some historical and political parameters for the use of the term so that political priorities can be established and different forms and degrees of suffering can be given the most attention.

A central tenet of modern feminist thought has been the assertion that "all women are oppressed." This assertion implies that women share a common lot, that factors like class, race, religion, sexual preference, etc. do not create a diversity of experience that determines the extent to which sexism will be an oppressive force in the lives of individual women. Sexism as a system of domination is institutionalized, but it has never determined in an absolute way the fate of all women in this society. Being oppressed means the *absence of choices*. It is the primary point of contact between the oppressed and the oppressor. Many women in this society do have choices (as inadequate as they are); therefore exploitation and discrimination are words that more accurately describe the lot of women collectively in the United States. Many women do not join organized resistance against sexism precisely because sexism has not meant an absolute lack of choices. They may know they are discriminated against on the basis of sex, but they do not equate this with oppression. Under capitalism, patriarchy is structured so that sexism restricts women's behavior in some realms even as freedom from limitations is allowed in other spheres. The absence of extreme restrictions leads many women to ignore the areas in which they are exploited or discriminated against; it may even lead them to imagine that no women are oppressed.

There are oppressed women in the United States, and it is both appropriate and necessary that we speak against such oppression. French feminist Christine Delphy makes the point in her essay "For a Materialist Feminism" that the use of the term "oppression" is important because it places feminist struggle in a radical political framework (a fuller discussion of Christine Delphy's perspective may be found in the collected essays of her work, *Close to Home*):

> The rebirth of feminism coincided with the use of the term "oppression." The ruling ideology, i.e. common sense, daily speech, does not speak about oppression but about a "feminine condition." It refers back to a naturalist explanation: to a constraint of nature, exterior reality out of reach and not modifiable by human action. The term "oppression," on the contrary, refers back to a choice, an explanation, a situation that is political. "Oppression" and "social oppression" are therefore synonyms, or rather social oppression is a redundance: the notion of a political origin, i.e. social, is an integral part of the concept of oppression.

However, feminist emphasis on "common oppression" in the United States was less a strategy for politicization than an appropriation by conservative and liberal women of a radical political vocabulary that masked the extent to which they shaped the movement so that it addressed and promoted their class interests.

Although the impulse towards unity and empathy that informed the notion of common oppression was directed at building solidarity, slogans like "organize around your own oppression" provided the excuse many privileged women needed to ignore the differences between their social status and the status of masses of women. It was a mark of race and class privilege, as well as the expression of freedom from the many constraints sexism places on working-class women, that middle-class white women were able to make their interests the primary focus of feminist movement and employ a rhetoric of commonality that made their condition synonymous with "oppression." Who was there to demand a change in vocabulary? What other group of women in the United States had the same access to universities, publishing houses, mass media, money? Had middle-class black women begun a movement in which they had labeled themselves "oppressed," no one would have taken them seriously. Had they established public forums and given speeches about their "oppression," they would have been criticized and attacked from all sides. This was not the case with white bourgeois feminists, for they could appeal to a large audience of women like themselves who were eager to change their lot in life. Their isolation from women of other class and race groups provided no immediate comparative base by which to test their assumptions of common oppression.

Initially, radical participants in women's movement demanded that women penetrate that isolation and create a space for contact. Anthologies like *Liberation Now!, Women's Liberation: Blueprint for the Future, Class and Feminism, Radical Feminism,* and *Sisterhood Is Powerful,* all published in the early 1970s, contain articles that attempted to address a wide audience of women, an audience that was not exclusively white, middle-class, college-educated, and adult (many have articles on teenagers). Sookie Stambler articulated this radical spirit in her introduction to *Women's Liberation: Blueprint for the Future:*

> Movement women have always been turned off by the media's necessity to create celebrities and superstars. This goes against our basic philosophy. We cannot relate to women in our ranks towering over us with prestige and fame. We are not struggling for the benefit of the one woman or for one group of women. We are dealing with issues that concern all women.

These sentiments, shared by many feminists early in the movement, were not sustained. As more and more women acquired prestige, fame, or money from feminist writings or from gains from feminist movement for equality in the work force, individual opportunism undermined appeals for collective struggle. Women who were not opposed to patriarchy, capitalism, classism, or racism labeled themselves "feminist." Their expectations were varied. Privileged women wanted social equality with men of their class; some women wanted equal pay for equal work; others wanted an alternative lifestyle. Many of these legitimate concerns were easily co-opted

by the ruling capitalist patriarchy. French feminist Antoinette
Fouque states:

> The actions proposed by the feminist groups are spectacular, pro-
> voking. But provocation only brings to light a certain number of
> social contradictions. It does not reveal radical contradictions
> within society. The feminists claim that they do not seek equality
> with men, but their practice proves the contrary to be true. Femi-
> nists are a bourgeois avant-garde that maintains, in an inverted
> form, the dominant values. Inversion does not facilitate the pas-
> sage to another kind of structure. Reformism suits everyone!
> Bourgeois order, capitalism, phallocentrism are ready to integrate
> as many feminists as will be necessary. Since these women are be-
> coming men, in the end it will only mean a few more men. The
> difference between the sexes is not whether one does or doesn't
> have a penis, it is whether or not one is an integral part of a phallic
> masculine economy.

Feminists in the United States are aware of the contradictions.
Carol Ehrlich makes the point in her essay "The Unhappy Marriage
of Marxism and Feminism: Can It Be Saved?" that "feminism seems
more and more to have taken on a blind, safe, nonrevolutionary out-
look" as "feminist radicalism loses ground to bourgeois feminism,"
stressing that "we cannot let this continue":

> Women need to know (and are increasingly prevented from find-
> ing out) that feminism is *not* about dressing for success, or be-
> coming a corporate executive, or gaining elective office; it is *not*
> being able to share a two-career marriage and take skiing vaca-
> tions and spend huge amounts of time with your husband and
> two lovely children because you have a domestic worker who
> makes all this possible for you, but who hasn't the time or money
> to do it for herself; it is *not* opening a Women's Bank, or spending
> a weekend in an expensive workshop that guarantees to teach you
> how to become assertive (but not aggressive); it is most emphati-
> cally *not* about becoming a police detective or CIA agent or ma-
> rine corps general.
>
> But if these distorted images of feminism have more reality
> than ours do, it is partly our own fault. We have not worked as

hard as we should have at providing clear and meaningful alternative analyses which relate to people's lives, and at providing active, accessible groups in which to work.

It is no accident that feminist struggle has been so easily co-opted to serve the interests of conservative and liberal feminists, since feminism in the United States has so far been a bourgeois ideology. Zillah Eisenstein discusses the liberal roots of North American feminism in *The Radical Future of Liberal Feminism,* explaining in the introduction:

> One of the major contributions to be found in this study is the role of the ideology of liberal individualism in the construction of feminist theory. Today's feminists either do not discuss a theory of individuality or they unself-consciously adopt the competitive, atomistic ideology of liberal individualism. There is much confusion on this issue in the feminist theory we discuss here. Until a conscious differentiation is made between a theory of individuality that recognizes the importance of the individual within the social collectivity and the ideology of individualism that assumes a competitive view of the individual, there will not be a full accounting of what a feminist theory of liberation must look like in our Western society.

The ideology of "competitive, atomistic...liberal individualism" has permeated feminist thought to such an extent that it undermines the potential radicalism of feminist struggle. The usurpation of feminism by bourgeois women to support their class interests has been to a very grave extent justified by feminist theory as it has so far been conceived (for example, the ideology of "common oppression"). Any movement to resist the co-optation of feminist struggle must begin by introducing a different feminist perspective—a new theory—one that is not informed by the ideology of liberal individualism.

The exclusionary practices of women who dominate feminist discourse have made it practically impossible for new and varied theories to emerge. Feminism has its party line, and women who feel a need for a different strategy, a different foundation, often find themselves ostracized and silenced. Criticisms of or alternatives to established feminist ideas are not encouraged, e.g. recent controversies about expanding feminist discussions of sexuality. Yet groups of women who feel excluded from feminist discourse and praxis can make a place for themselves only if they first create, via critiques, an awareness of the factors that alienate them. Many individual white women found in the women's movement a liberatory solution to personal dilemmas. Having directly benefited from the movement, they are less inclined to criticize it or to engage in rigorous examination of its structure than those who feel it has not had a revolutionary impact on their lives or the lives of masses of women in our society. Non-white women who feel affirmed within the current structure of feminist movement (even though they may form autonomous groups) seem also to feel that their definitions of the party line, whether on the issue of black feminism or on other issues, are the only legitimate discourse. Rather than encourage a diversity of voices, critical dialogue, and controversy, they, like some white women, seek to stifle dissent. As activists and writers whose work is widely known, they act as if they are best able to judge whether other women's voices should be heard. Susan Griffin warns against this overall tendency towards dogmatism in her essay "The Way of All Ideology":

> When a theory is transformed into an ideology, it begins to destroy the self and self-knowledge. Originally born of feeling, it pretends to float above and around feeling. Above sensation. It organizes experience according to itself, without touching experience. By virtue of being itself, it is supposed to know. To invoke the name of this ideology is to confer truthfulness. No one can tell it anything new. Experience ceases to surprise it, inform it, transform it. It is annoyed by any detail which does not fit into its world view. Begun as a cry against the denial of truth, now it denies any truth which does not fit into its scheme. Begun as a way to restore one's sense of reality, now it attempts to discipline real people, to remake natural beings after its own image. All that it fails to explain it records as its enemy. Begun as a theory of liberation, it is threatened by new theories of liberation; it builds a prison for the mind.

We resist hegemonic dominance of feminist thought by insisting that it is a theory in the making, that we must necessarily criticize, question, re-examine, and explore new possibilities. My persistent critique has been informed by my status as a member of an oppressed group, my experience of sexist exploitation and discrimination, and the sense that prevailing feminist analysis has not been the force shaping my feminist consciousness. This is true for many women. There are white women who had never considered resisting male dominance until the feminist movement created an awareness that could and should. My awareness of feminist struggle was stimulated by social circumstance. Growing up in a Southern, black, father-dominated, working-class household, I experienced (as did my mother, my sisters, and my brother) varying degrees of patriarchal tyranny, and it made me angry—it made us all angry. Anger led me to question the politics of male dominance and enabled me to resist sexist socialization. Frequently, white feminists act as if black women did not know sexist oppression existed until they voiced feminist sentiment. They believe they are providing black women with "the" analysis and "the" program for liberation. They do not understand, cannot even imagine, that black women, as well as other groups of women who live daily in oppressive situations, often acquire an awareness of patriarchal politics from their lived experience, just as they develop strategies of resistance (even though they may not resist on a sustained or organized basis).

These black women observed white feminist focus on male tyranny and women's oppression as if it were a "new" revelation, and felt such a focus had little impact on their lives. To them it was just another indication of the privileged living conditions of middle- and upper-class white women that they would need a theory to "inform them that they were oppressed." The implication being that people who are truly oppressed know it even though they may not be engaged in organized resistance or are unable to articulate in written form the nature of their oppression. These black women saw nothing liberatory in party-line analyses of women's oppression. Neither the fact that black women have not organized collectively in huge numbers around the issues of "feminism" (many of us do not know or use the term) nor the fact that we have not had access to the machinery of power that would allow us to share our analyses or theories about gender with the American public negates its presence in our lives or places us in a position of dependency in relationship to those white and non-white feminists who address a larger audience.

The understanding I had by age thirteen of patriarchal politics created in me expectations of the feminist movement that were quite different from those of young, middle-class white women. When I entered my first women's studies class at Stanford University in the early 1970s, white women were reveling in the joy of being together—to them it was an important, momentous occasion. I had not known a life where women had not been together, where women had not helped, protected, and loved one another deeply. I had not known white women who were ignorant of the impact of race and class on their social status and consciousness. (Southern white women often have a more realistic perspective on racism and classism than white women in other areas of the United States.) I did not feel sympathetic to white peers who maintained that I could not expect them to have knowledge of or understand the life experiences of black women. Despite my background (living in racially segregated communities) I knew about the lives of white women, and certainly no white women lived in our neighborhood, attended our schools, or worked in our homes.

When I participated in feminist groups, I found that white women adopted a condescending attitude towards me and other non-white participants. The condescension they directed at black women was one of the means they employed to remind us that the women's movement was "theirs"—that we were able to participate because they allowed it, even encouraged it; after all, we were needed to legitimate the process. They did not see us as equals. They did not treat us as equals. And though they expected us to provide first-hand accounts of black experience, they felt it was their role to decide if these experiences were authentic. Frequently, college-educated black women (even those from poor and working-class backgrounds) were dismissed as mere imitators. Our presence in movement activities did not count, as white women were convinced that "real" blackness meant speaking the patois of poor black people, being uneducated, streetwise, and a variety of other stereotypes. If we dared to criticize the movement or to assume responsibility for re-shaping feminist ideas and introducing new ideas, our voices were tuned out, dismissed, silenced. We could be heard only if our state-ments echoed the sentiments of the dominant discourse.

Attempts by white feminists to silence black women are rarely written about. All too often they have taken place in conference rooms, classrooms, or the privacy of cozy living-room settings, where one lone black woman faces the racist hostility of a group of white women. From the time the women's liberation movement be-gan, individual black women went to groups. Many never returned after a first meeting. Anita Cornwell is correct in "Three for the Price of One: Notes from a Gay Black Feminist" when she states, "Sadly enough, fear of encountering racism seems to be one of the main reasons that so many black women refuse to join the women's movement." Recent focus on the issue of racism has generated dis-course but has had little impact on the behavior of white feminists towards black women. Often the white women who are busy pub-lishing papers and books on "unlearning racism" remain patroniz-ing and condescending when they relate to black women. This is not surprising given that frequently their discourse is aimed solely in the direction of a white audience and the focus solely on changing atti-tudes rather than addressing racism in a historical and political con-text. They make us the "objects" of their privileged discourse on race. As "objects," we remain unequals, inferiors. Even though they may be sincerely concerned about racism, their methodology sug-gests they are not yet free of the type of paternalism endemic to white supremacist ideology. Some of these women place themselves in the position of "authorities" who must mediate communication between racist white women (naturally they see themselves as hav-ing come to terms with their racism) and angry black women whom they believe are incapable of rational discourse. Of course, the sys-tem of racism, classism, and educational elitism must remain intact if they are to maintain their authoritative positions.

In 1981, I enrolled in a graduate class on feminist theory where we were given a course reading list that had writings by white women and men and one black man, but no material by or about black, Native American Indian, Hispanic, or Asian women. When I criticized this oversight, white women directed an anger and hostility at me that was so intense I found it difficult to attend the class. When I suggested that the purpose of this collective anger was to create an atmosphere in which it would be psychologically unbearable for me to speak in class discussions or even attend class, I was told that they were not angry. *I* was the one who was angry. Weeks after class ended, I received an open letter from one white female student acknowledging her anger and expressing regret for her attacks. She wrote:

> I didn't know you. You were black. In class after a while I noticed myself, that I would always be the one to respond to whatever you said. And usually it was to contradict. Not that the argument was always about racism by any means. But I think the hidden logic was that if I could prove you wrong about one thing, then you might not be right about anything at all.

And in another paragraph:

> I said in class one day that there were some people less entrapped than others by Plato's picture of the world. I said I thought we, after fifteen years of education, courtesy of the ruling class, might be more entrapped than others who had not received a start in life so close to the heart of the monster. My classmate, once a close friend, sister, colleague, has not spoken to me since then. I think the possibility that we were not the best spokespeople for all women made her fear for her self-worth and for her Ph.D.

Often in situations where white feminists aggressively attacked individual black women, they saw themselves as the ones who were under attack, who were the victims. During a heated discussion with another white female student in a racially mixed women's group I had organized, I was told that she had heard how I had "wiped out" people in the feminist theory class, that she was afraid of being "wiped out," too. I reminded her that I was one person speaking to a large group of angry, aggressive people; I was hardly dominating the situation. It was I who left the class in tears, not any of the people I had supposedly "wiped out."

Racist stereotypes of the strong, superhuman black woman are operative myths in the minds of many white women, allowing them to ignore the extent to which black women are likely to be victimized in this society, and the role white women may play in the maintenance and perpetuation of that victimization. In Lillian Hellman's autobiographical work *Pentimento,* she writes, "All my life, beginning at birth, I have taken orders from black women, wanting them and resenting them, being superstitious the few times I disobeyed." The black women Hellman describes worked in her household as family servants, and their status was never that of an equal. Even as a child, she was always in the dominant position as they questioned, advised, or guided her; they were free to exercise these rights because she or another white authority figure allowed it. Hellman places power in the hands of these black women rather than acknowledge her own power over them; hence she mystifies the true nature of their relationship. By projecting onto black women a mythical power and strength, white women both promote a false image of themselves as powerless, passive victims and deflect attention away from their aggressiveness, their power (however limited in a white supremacist, male-dominated state), their willingness to dominate and control others. These unacknowledged aspects of the social status of many white women prevent them from transcending racism and limit the scope of their understanding of women's overall social status in the United States.

Privileged feminists have largely been unable to speak to, with, and for diverse groups of women because they either do not understand fully the interrelatedness of sex, race, and class oppression or refuse to take this interrelatedness seriously. Feminist analyses of woman's lot tend to focus exclusively on gender and do not provide a solid foundation on which to construct feminist theory. They reflect the dominant tendency in Western patriarchal minds to mystify woman's reality by insisting that gender is the sole determinant of woman's fate. Certainly it has been easier for women who do not experience race or class oppression to focus exclusively on gender. Although socialist feminists focus on class and gender, they tend to dismiss race, or they make a point of acknowledging that race is important and then proceed to offer an analysis in which race is not considered.

As a group, black women are in an unusual position in this society, for not only are we collectively at the bottom of the occupational ladder, but our overall social status is lower than that of any other group. Occupying such a position, we bear the brunt of sexist, racist, and classist oppression. At the same time, we are the group that has not been socialized to assume the role of exploiter/oppressor in that we are allowed no institutionalized "other" that we can exploit or oppress. (Children do not represent an institutionalized other even though they may be oppressed by parents.) White women and black men have it both ways. They can act as oppressor or be oppressed. Black men may be victimized by racism, but sexism allows them to act as exploiters and oppressors of women. White women may be victimized by sexism, but racism enables them to act as exploiters and oppressors of black people. Both groups have led liberation movements that favor their interests and support the continued oppression of other groups. Black male sexism has undermined struggles to eradicate racism just as white female racism undermines feminist struggle. As long as these two groups, or any group, defines liberation as gaining social equality with ruling-class white men, they have a vested interest in the continued exploitation and oppression of others.

Black women with no institutionalized "other" that we may discriminate against, exploit, or oppress often have a lived experience that directly challenges the prevailing classist, sexist, racist social structure and its concomitant ideology. This lived experience may shape our consciousness in such a way that our world view differs from those who have a degree of privilege (however relative within the existing system). It is essential for continued feminist struggle that black women recognize the special vantage point our marginality gives us and make use of this perspective to criticize the dominant racist, classist, sexist hegemony as well as to envision and create a counter-hegemony. I am suggesting that we have a central role to play in the making of feminist theory and a contribution to offer that is unique and valuable. The formation of a liberatory feminist theory and praxis is a collective responsibility, one that must be shared. Though I criticize aspects of feminist movement as we have known it so far, a critique which is sometimes harsh and unrelenting, I do so not in an attempt to diminish feminist struggle but to enrich, to share in the work of making a liberatory ideology and a liberatory movement.

2

FEMINISM
A Movement
to End Sexist Oppression

A central problem within feminist discourse has been our inability to either arrive at a consensus of opinion about what feminism is or accept definition(s) that could serve as points of unification. Without agreed-upon definition(s), we lack a sound foundation on which to construct theory or engage in overall meaningful praxis. Expressing her frustrations with the absence of clear definitions in a recent essay, "Towards a Revolutionary Ethics," Carmen Vazquez comments:

> We can't even agree on what a "Feminist" is, never mind what she would believe in and how she defines the principles that consti- tute honor among us. In key with the American capitalist obses- sion for individualism and anything goes so long as it gets you what you want, feminism in America has come to mean anything you like, honey. There are as many definitions of Feminism as there are feminists, some of my sisters say, with a chuckle. I don't think it's funny.

It is not funny. It indicates a growing lack of interest in feminism as a radical political movement. It is a despairing gesture expressive of the belief that solidarity among women is not possible. It is a sign that the political naïveté which has traditionally characterized woman's lot in male-dominated culture abounds.

Most people in the United States think of feminism, or the more commonly used term "women's lib," as a movement that aims to make women the social equals of men. This broad definition, popularized by the media and mainstream segments of the movement, raises problematic questions. Since men are not equals in white supremacist, capitalist, patriarchal class structure, which men do women want to be equal to? Do women share a common vision of what equality means? Implicit in this simplistic definition of women's liberation is a dismissal of race and class as factors that, in conjunction with sexism, determine the extent to which an individual will be discriminated against, exploited, or oppressed. Bourgeois white women interested in women's rights issues have been satisfied with simple definitions for obvious reasons. Rhetorically placing themselves in the same social category as oppressed women, they are not anxious to call attention to race and class privilege.

Women in lower-class and poor groups, particularly those who are non-white, would not have defined women's liberation as women gaining social equality with men, since they are continually reminded in their everyday lives that all women do not share a common social status. Concurrently, they know that many males in their social groups are exploited and oppressed. Knowing that men in their groups do not have social, political, and economic power, they would not deem it liberatory to share their social status. While they are aware that sexism enables men in their respective groups to have privileges that are denied them, they are more likely to see exaggerated expressions of male chauvinism among their peers as stemming from the male's sense of himself as powerless and ineffectual in relation to ruling male groups, rather than an expression of an overall privileged social status. From the very onset of the women's liberation movement, these women were suspicious of feminism precisely because they recognized the limitations inherent in its definition. They recognized the possibility that feminism defined as social equality with men might easily become a movement that would primarily affect the social standing of white women in middle- and upper-class groups while affecting only in a very marginal way the social status of working-class and poor women.

Not all the women who were at the forefront of organized women's movement, shaping definitions, were content with making women's liberation synonymous with women gaining social equality with men. On the opening pages of *Woman Power: The Movement for Women's Liberation,* Cellestine Ware, a black woman active in the movement, wrote under the heading "Goals":

> Radical feminism is working for the eradication of domination and elitism in all human relationships. This would make self-determination the ultimate good and require the downfall of society as we know it today.

Individual radical feminists like Charlotte Bunch based their analyses on an informed understanding of the politics of domination and a recognition of the interconnections among various systems of domination even as they focused primarily on sexism. Their perspectives were not valued by those organizers and participants in women's movement who were more interested in social reforms. The anonymous authors of a pamphlet on feminist issues published in 1976, *Women and the New World,* make the point that many women active in women's liberation movement were far more comfortable with the notion of feminism as a reform that would help women attain social equality with men of their class than feminism defined as a radical movement that would eradicate domination and transform society:

> Whatever the organization, the location, or the ethnic composition of the group, all the women's liberation organizations had one thing in common: they all came together based on a biological and sociological fact rather than on a body of ideas. Women came together in the women's liberation movement on the basis that we were women and all women are subject to male domination. We saw all women as being our allies and all men as being the oppressor. We never questioned the extent to which American women accept the same materialistic and individualistic values as American men. We did not stop to think that American women are just as reluctant as American men to struggle for a new society based on new values of mutual respect, cooperation and social responsibility.

It is now evident that many women active in feminist movement were interested in reform as an end in itself, not as a stage in the progression towards revolutionary transformation. Even though Zillah Eisenstein can optimistically point to the potential radicalism of liberal women who work for social reform in *The Radical Future of Liberal Feminism,* the process by which this radicalism will surface is unclear. Eisenstein offers as an example of the radical implications of liberal feminist programs the demands made at the government-sponsored Houston conference on women's rights issues which took place in 1978:

> The Houston report demands as a human right a full voice and role for women in determining the destiny of our world, our nation, our families, and our individual lives. It specifically calls for (1) the elimination of violence in the home and the development of shelters for battered women, (2) support for women's business, (3) a solution to child abuse, (4) federally funded nonsexist child care, (5) a policy of full employment so that all women who wish and are able to work may do so, (6) the protection of homemakers so that marriage is a partnership, (7) an end to the sexist portrayal of women in the media, (8) establishment of reproductive freedom and the end to involuntary sterilization, (9) a remedy to the double discrimination against minority women, (10) a revision of criminal codes dealing with rape, (11) elimination of discrimination on the basis of sexual preference, (12) the establishment of nonsexist education, and (13) an examination of all welfare reform proposals for their specific impact on women.

The positive impact of liberal reforms on women's lives should not lead to the assumption that they eradicate systems of domination. Nowhere in these demands is there an emphasis on eradicating the politic of domination, yet it would need to be abolished if any of these demands were to be met. The lack of any emphasis on domination is consistent with the liberal feminist belief that women can achieve equality with men of their class without challenging and changing the cultural basis of group oppression. It is this belief that negates the likelihood that the potential radicalism of liberal feminism will ever be realized. Writing as early as 1967, Brazilian scholar Heleieth Saffioti emphasized that bourgeois feminism has always been "fundamentally and unconsciously a feminism of the ruling class," that:

> Whatever revolutionary content there is in petty-bourgeois femi-
> nist praxis, it has been put there by the efforts of the middle
> strata, especially the less well-off, to move up socially. To do this,
> however, they sought merely to expand the existing social struc-
> tures, and never went so far as to challenge the status quo. Thus,
> while petty-bourgeois feminism may always have aimed at estab-
> lishing social equality between the sexes, the consciousness it rep-
> resented has remained utopian in its desire for and struggle to
> bring about a partial transformation of society; this, it believed,
> could be done without disturbing the foundations on which it
> rested.... In this sense, petty-bourgeois feminism is not feminism
> at all; indeed it has helped to consolidate class society by giving
> camouflage to its internal contradictions.

Radical dimensions of liberal women's social protest will continue to serve as an ideological support system providing the necessary
critical and analytical impetus for the maintenance of a liberalism
that aims to grant women greater equality of opportunity within the
present white supremacist, capitalist, patriarchal state. Such liberal
women's rights activism in its essence diminishes feminist struggle.
Philosopher Mihailo Markovic discusses the limitations of liberalism in his essay "Women's Liberation and Human Emancipation":

> Another basic characteristic of liberalism which constitutes a for-
> midable obstacle to an oppressed social group's emancipation is
> its conception of human nature. If selfishness, aggressiveness, the
> drive to conquer and dominate, really are among defining human
> traits, as every liberal philosopher since Locke tries to convince
> us, the oppression in civil society—i.e. in the social sphere not
> regulated by the state—is a fact of life, and the basic civil relation-
> ship between a man and a woman will always remain a battlefield.
> Woman, being less aggressive, is then either the less human of the
> two and doomed to subjugation, or else she must get more
> power-hungry herself and try to dominate man. Liberation for
> both is not feasible.

Although liberal perspectives on feminism include reforms that would have radical implications for society, these are the reforms that will be resisted precisely because they would set the stage for revolutionary transformation were they implemented. It is evident that society is more responsive to those "feminist" demands that are not threatening, that may even help maintain the status quo. Jeanne Gross gives an example of this co-optation of feminist strategy in her essay "Feminist Ethics from a Marxist Perspective," published in 1977:

> If we as women want change in all aspects of our lives, we must recognize that capitalism is uniquely capable of co-opting piece-meal change…. Capitalism is capable of taking our visionary changes and using them against us. For example, many married women, recognizing their oppression in the family, have divorced. They are thrown, with no preparation or protection, into the la-bor market. For many women this has meant taking their places at the row of typewriters. Corporations are now recognizing the capacity for exploitation in divorced women. The turnover in such jobs is incredibly high. "If she complains, she can be replaced."

Particularly as regards work, many liberal feminist reforms simply reinforced capitalist, materialist values (illustrating the flexibility of capitalism) without truly liberating women economically.

Liberal women have not been alone in drawing upon the dyna-mism of feminism to further their interests. The great majority of women who have benefited in any way from feminist-generated so-cial reforms do not want to be seen as advocates of feminism. Con-ferences on issues of relevance to women, which would never have been organized or funded had there not been a feminist movement, take place all over the United States, and the participants do not want to be seen as advocates of feminism. They are either reluctant to make a public commitment to feminist movement or they sneer at the term. Individual African American, Native American Indian, Asian American, and Hispanic American women find themselves isolated if they support feminist movement. Even women who may achieve fame and notoriety (as well as increased economic income) in response to attention given their work by large numbers of women who support feminism may deflect attention away from their engagement with feminist movement. They may even go so far as to create other terms that express their concern with women's issues so as to avoid using the term "feminist." The creation of new terms that have no relationship to organized political activity tends to provide women who may already be reluctant to explore feminism with ready excuses to explain their reluctance to participate. This illustrates an uncritical acceptance of distorted definitions of feminism rather than a demand for redefinition. Women may support specific issues while divorcing themselves from what they assume is feminist movement.

In an article, "Sisters—Under the Skin," in a San Francisco newspaper, columnist Bob Greene commented on the aversion many women apparently have to the term "feminism." Greene finds it curious that many women "who obviously believe in everything that proud feminists believe in dismiss the term 'feminist' as something unpleasant; something with which they do not wish to be associated." Even though such women often acknowledge that they have benefited from feminist-generated reform measures that have improved the social status of specific groups of women, they do not wish to be seen as participants in feminist movement:

> There is no getting around it. After all this time, the term "feminist" makes many bright, ambitious, intelligent women embarrassed and uncomfortable. They simply don't want to be associated with it.
>
> It's as if it has an unpleasant connotation that they want no connection with. Chances are if you were to present them with every mainstream feminist belief, they would go along with the beliefs to the letter—and even if they consider themselves feminists, they hasten to say no.

Many women are reluctant to advocate feminism because they are uncertain about the meaning of the term. Other women from exploited and oppressed ethnic groups dismiss the term because they do not wish to be perceived as supporting a racist movement; feminism is often equated with white women's rights efforts. Large numbers of women see feminism as synonymous with lesbianism; their homophobia leads them to reject association with any group identified as pro-lesbian. Some women fear the word "feminism" because they shun identification with any political movement, especially one perceived as radical. Of course there are women who do not wish to be associated with women's rights movement in any form, so they reject and oppose feminist movement. Most women are more familiar with negative perspectives on "women's lib" than with the positive significations of feminism. It is this term's positive political significance and power that we must now struggle to recover and maintain.

Currently feminism seems to be a term without any clear significance. The "anything goes" approach to the definition of the word has rendered it practically meaningless. What is meant by "anything goes" is usually that any woman who wants social equality with men regardless of her political perspective (she can be a conservative right-winger or a nationalist communist) can label herself feminist. Most attempts at defining feminism reflect the class nature of the movement. Definitions are usually liberal in origin and focus on the individual woman's right to freedom and self-determination. In Barbara Berg's *The Remembered Gate: Origins of American Feminism,* she defines feminism as a "broad movement embracing numerous phases of woman's emancipation." However, her emphasis is on women gaining greater individual freedom. Expanding on the above definition, Berg adds:

> It is the freedom to decide her own destiny; freedom from x-determined role; freedom from society's oppressive restrictions; freedom to express her thoughts fully and to convert them freely into action. Feminism demands the acceptance of woman's right to individual conscience and judgment. It postulates that woman's essential worth stems from her common humanity and does not depend on the other relationships of her life.

This definition of feminism is almost apolitical in tone; yet it is the type of definition many liberal women find appealing. It evokes a very romantic notion of personal freedom that is more acceptable than a definition that emphasizes radical political action.

Many feminist radicals now know that neither a feminism that focuses on woman as an autonomous human being worthy of personal freedom nor one that focuses on the attainment of equality of opportunity with men can rid society of sexism and male domination. Feminism is a struggle to end sexist oppression. Therefore, it is necessarily a struggle to eradicate the ideology of domination that permeates Western culture on various levels, as well as a commitment to reorganizing society so that the self-development of people can take precedence over imperialism, economic expansion, and material desires. Defined in this way, it is unlikely that women would join feminist movement simply because we are biologically the same. A commitment to feminism so defined would demand that each individual participant acquire a critical political consciousness based on ideas and beliefs.

Over time the slogan "the personal is political" (which was first used to stress that woman's everyday reality is informed and shaped by politics and is necessarily political) became a means of encouraging women to think that the experience of discrimination, exploitation, or oppression automatically corresponded with an understanding of the ideological and institutional apparatus shaping one's social status. As a consequence, many women who had not fully examined their situation never developed a sophisticated understanding of their political reality and its relationship to that of women as a collective group. They were encouraged to focus on giving voice to personal experience. Like revolutionaries working to change the lot of colonized people globally, it is necessary for feminist activists to stress that the ability to see and describe one's own reality is a significant step in the long process of self-recovery, but it is only a beginning. When women internalized the idea that describing their own woe was synonymous with developing a critical political consciousness, the progress of feminist movement was stalled. Starting from such incomplete perspectives, it is not surprising that theories and strategies were developed that were collectively inadequate and misguided. To correct this inadequacy in past analysis, we must now encourage women to develop a keen, comprehensive understanding of women's political reality. Broader perspectives can only emerge as we examine both the personal that is political, the politics of society as a whole, and global revolutionary politics.

Feminism defined in political terms that stress collective as well as individual experience challenges women to enter a new domain—to leave behind the apolitical stance sexism decrees is our lot and develop political consciousness. Women know from our everyday lives that many of us rarely discuss politics. Even when women talked about sexist politics in the heyday of contemporary feminism, rather than allow this engagement with serious political matters to lead to complex, in-depth analysis of women's social status, we insisted that men were "the enemy," the cause of all our problems. As a consequence, we examined almost exclusively women's relationship to male supremacy and the ideology of sexism. The focus on "man as enemy" created, as Marlene Dixon emphasizes in her essay "The Rise and Demise of Women's Liberation: A Class Analysis," a "politics of psychological oppression" that evoked world views that "pit individual against individual and mystify the social basis of exploitation." By repudiating the popular notion that the focus of feminist movement should be social equality of the sexes and by emphasizing eradication of the cultural basis of group oppression, our own analysis would require an exploration of all aspects of women's political reality. This would mean that race and class oppression would be recognized as feminist issues with as much relevance as sexism.

When feminism is defined in such a way that it calls attention to the diversity of women's social and political reality, it centralizes the experiences of all women, especially the women whose social conditions have been least written about, studied, or changed by political movements. When we cease to focus on the simplistic stance "men are the enemy," we are compelled to examine systems of domination and our role in their maintenance and perpetuation. Lack of adequate definition made it easy for bourgeois women, whether liberal or radical in perspective, to maintain their dominance over the leadership of the movement and its direction. This hegemony continues to exist in most feminist organizations. Exploited and oppressed groups of women are usually encouraged by those in power to feel that their situation is hopeless, that they can do nothing to break the pattern of domination. Given such socialization, these women have often felt that our only response to white, bourgeois, hegemonic dominance of feminist movement is to trash, reject, or dismiss feminism. This reaction is in no way threatening to the women who wish to maintain control over the direction of feminist theory and praxis. They prefer us to be silent, passively accepting their ideas. They prefer us speaking against "them" rather than developing our own ideas about feminist movement.

Feminism is the struggle to end sexist oppression. Its aim is not to benefit solely any specific group of women, any particular race or class of women. It does not privilege women over men. It has the power to transform in a meaningful way all our lives. Most importantly, feminism is neither a lifestyle nor a ready-made identity or role one can step into. Diverting energy from feminist movement that aims to change society, many women concentrate on the development of a counter-culture, a woman-centered world wherein participants have little contact with men. Such attempts do not indicate a respect or concern for the vast majority of women who are unable to integrate their cultural expressions with the visions offered by alternative, woman-centered communities. In *Beyond God the Father,* Mary Daly urged women to give up "the securities offered by the patriarchal system" and create new space that would be woman-centered. Responding to Daly, Jeanne Gross pointed to the contradictions that arise when the focus of feminist movement is on the construction of new space:

> Creating a "counterworld" places an incredible amount of pressure on the women who attempt to embark on such a project. The pressure comes from the belief that the only true resources for such an endeavor are ourselves. The past which is totally patriarchal is viewed as irredeemable....
>
> If we go about creating an alternative culture without remaining in dialogue with others (and the historical circumstances that give rise to their identity) we have no reality check for our goals. We run the very real risk that the dominant ideology of the culture is re-duplicated in the feminist movement through cultural imperialism.

Equating feminist struggle with living in a counter-cultural, woman-centered world erected barriers that closed the movement off from most women. Despite sexist discrimination, exploitation, or oppression, many women feel their lives as they live them are important and valuable. Naturally the suggestion that these lives could be simply left or abandoned for an alternative "feminist" lifestyle met with resistance. Feeling their life experiences devalued, deemed solely negative and worthless, many women responded by vehemently attacking feminism. By rejecting the notion of an alternative feminist "lifestyle" that can emerge only when women create a subculture (whether it is living space or even space like women's studies, which on many campuses has become exclusive), and by insisting that feminist struggle can begin wherever an individual woman is, we create a movement that focuses on our collective experience, a movement that is continually mass-based.

Over the past six years, many separatist-oriented communities have been formed by women so that the focus has shifted from the development of woman-centered space towards an emphasis on identity. Once woman-centered space exists, it can be maintained only if women remain convinced that it is the only place where they can be self-realized and free. After assuming a "feminist" identity, women often seek to live the "feminist" lifestyle. These women do not see that it undermines feminist movement to project the assumption that "feminist" is but another pre-packaged role women can now select as they search for identity. The willingness to see feminism as a lifestyle choice rather than a political commitment reflects the class nature of the movement. It is not surprising that the vast majority of women who equate feminism with alternative lifestyle are from middle-class backgrounds, unmarried, college-educated, often students who are without many of the social and economic responsibilities that working-class and poor women who are laborers, parents, homemakers, and wives confront daily. Sometimes lesbians have sought to equate feminism with lifestyle, but for significantly different reasons. Given the prejudice and discrimination against lesbian women in our society, alternative communities that are woman-centered are one means of creating positive, affirming environments. Despite positive reasons for developing woman-centered space (which does not need to be equated with a "feminist" lifestyle), like pleasure, support, and resource-sharing, emphasis on creating a counter-culture has alienated women from feminist movement, for such space can be in churches, kitchens, etc.

Longing for community, connection, a sense of shared purpose, many women found support networks in feminist organizations. Satisfied in a personal way by new relationships generated in what was called a "safe," "supportive" context wherein discussion focused on feminist ideology, they did not question whether masses of women shared the same need for community. Certainly many black women as well as women from other ethnic groups do not feel an absence of community among women in their lives, despite exploitation and oppression. The focus on feminism as a way to develop shared identity and community has little appeal to women who experience community, who seek ways to end exploitation and oppression in the context of their lives. While they may develop an interest in a feminist politic that works to eradicate sexist oppression, they will probably never feel as intense a need for a "feminist" identity and lifestyle.

Often emphasis on identity and lifestyle is appealing because it creates a false sense that one is engaged in praxis. However, praxis within any political movement that aims to have a radical transformative impact on society cannot be solely focused on creating spaces wherein would-be radicals experience safety and support. Feminist movement to end sexist oppression actively engages participants in revolutionary struggle. Struggle is rarely safe or pleasurable.

Focusing on feminism as political commitment, we resist the emphasis on individual identity and lifestyle. (This should not be confused with the very real need to unite theory and practice.) Such resistance engages us in revolutionary praxis. The ethics of Western society informed by imperialism and capitalism are personal rather than social. They teach us that the individual good is more important than the collective good, and consequently that individual change is of greater significance than collective change. This particular form of cultural imperialism has been reproduced in feminist movement in the form of individual women equating the fact that their lives have been changed in a meaningful way by feminism "as is" with a policy that no change need occur in the theory and praxis, even if it has little or no impact on society as a whole, or on masses of women.

To emphasize that engagement with feminist struggle as political commitment, we could avoid using the phrase "I am a feminist" (a linguistic structure designed to refer to some personal aspect of identity and self-definition) and could state, "I advocate feminism." Because there has been undue emphasis placed on feminism as an identity or lifestyle, people usually resort to stereotyped perspectives on feminism. Deflecting attention away from stereotypes is necessary if we are to revise our strategy and direction. I have found that saying "I am a feminist" usually means I am plugged into preconceived notions of identity, role, or behavior. When I say, "I advocate feminism," the response is usually, "What is feminism?" A phrase like "I advocate" does not imply the kind of absolutism that is suggested by "I am." It does not engage us in the either/or dualistic thinking that is the central ideological component of all systems of domination in Western society. It implies that a choice has been made, that commitment to feminism is an act of will. It does not suggest that by committing oneself to feminism, the possibility of supporting other political movements is negated.

As a black woman interested in feminist movement, I am often asked whether being black is more important than being a woman; whether feminist struggle to end sexist oppression is more important than the struggle to end racism or vice versa. All such questions are rooted in competitive either/or thinking, the belief that the self is formed in opposition to an other. Therefore one is a feminist because one is not something else. Most people are socialized to think in terms of opposition rather than compatibility. Rather than seeing anti-racist work as totally compatible with working to end sexist oppression, they often see them as two movements competing for first place. When one is asked, "Are you a feminist?," it appears that an affirmative answer is translated to mean that one is concerned with no political issues other than feminism. When one is black, an affir-

mative response is likely to be heard as a devaluation of struggle to
end racism. Given the fear of being misunderstood, it has been difficult for black women and women in exploited and oppressed ethnic
groups to give expression to their interest in feminist concerns.
They have been wary of saying "I am a feminist." The shift in expression from "I am a feminist" to "I advocate feminism" could
serve as a useful strategy for eliminating the focus on identity and
lifestyle. It could serve as a way in which women who are concerned
about feminism as well as other political movements could express
their support while avoiding linguistic structures that give primacy
to one particular group. It would also encourage greater exploration
in feminist theory.

The shift in definition away from notions of social equality towards an emphasis on ending sexist oppression leads to a shift in attitudes in regard to the development of theory. Given the class
nature of feminist movement so far, as well as racial hierarchies, developing theory (the guiding set of beliefs and principles that becomes the basis for action) has been a task particularly subject to the
hegemonic dominance of white academic women. This has led
many women outside the privileged race/class group to see the focus on developing theory, even the very use of the term, as a concern
that functions only to reinforce the power of the elite group. Such
reactions reinforce the sexist/racist/classist notion that developing
theory is the domain of the white intellectual. Privileged white
women active in feminist movement, whether liberal or radical in
perspective, encourage black women to contribute "experiential"
work, personal life stories. Personal experiences are important to
feminist movement, but they cannot take the place of theory. Charlotte Bunch explains the special significance of theory in her essay
"Feminism and Education: Not by Degrees":

> Theory enables us to see immediate needs in terms of long-range
> goals and an overall perspective on the world. It thus gives us a
> framework for evaluating various strategies in both the long and
> the short run and for seeing the types of changes that they are
> likely to produce. Theory is not just a body of facts or a set of per-
> sonal opinions. It involves explanations and hypotheses that are

based on available knowledge and experience. It is also dependent on conjecture and insight about how to interpret those facts and experiences and their significance.

Since bourgeois white women had defined feminism in such a way as to make it appear that it had no real significance for black women, they could then conclude that black women need not contribute to developing theory. We were to provide the colorful life stories to document and validate the prevailing set of theoretical assumptions. (An interesting discussion of black women's responses to feminist movement may be found in the essay "Challenging Imperial Feminism" by Valerie Amos and Pratibha Parmar.) Focus on social equality with men as a definition of feminism led to an emphasis on discrimination, male attitudes, and legalistic reforms. Feminism as a movement to end sexist oppression directs our attention to systems of domination and the interrelatedness of sex, race, and class oppression. Therefore, it compels us to centralize the experiences and the social predicaments of women who bear the brunt of sexist oppression as a way to understand the collective social status of women in the United States. Defining feminism as a movement to end sexist oppression is crucial for the development of theory because it is a starting point indicating the direction of exploration and analysis.

The foundation of future feminist struggle must be solidly based on a recognition of the need to eradicate the underlying cultural basis and causes of sexism and other forms of group oppression. Without challenging and changing these philosophical structures, no feminist reforms will have a long-range impact. Consequently, it is now necessary for advocates of feminism to collectively acknowledge that our struggle cannot be defined as a movement to gain social equality with men, that terms like "liberal feminist" and "bourgeois feminist" represent contradictions that must be resolved so that feminism will not be continually co-opted to serve the opportunistic ends of special-interest groups.

3

THE SIGNIFICANCE
OF FEMINIST MOVEMENT

Contemporary feminist movement in the United States called attention to the exploitation and oppression of women globally. This was a major contribution to feminist struggle. In their eagerness to highlight sexist injustice, women focused almost exclusively on the ideology and practice of male domination. Unfortunately, this made it appear that feminism was more a declaration of war between the sexes than a political struggle to end sexist oppression, a struggle that would imply change on the part of women and men. Underlying much white women's liberationist rhetoric was the implication that men had nothing to gain by feminist movement, that its success would make them losers. Militant white women were particularly eager to make feminist movement privilege women over men. Their anger, hostility, and rage was so intense that they were unable to resist turning the movement into a public forum for their attacks. Although they sometimes considered themselves "radical feminists," their responses were reactionary. Fundamentally, they argued *that all men are the enemies of all women* and proposed as solutions to this problem a utopian woman nation, separatist communities, and even the subjugation or extermination of all men. Their anger may have been a catalyst for individual liberatory resistance and change. It may have encouraged bonding with other women to raise consciousness. It did not strengthen public understanding of the significance of authentic feminist movement.

Sexist discrimination, exploitation, and oppression have created the war between the sexes. Traditionally the battleground has been the home. In recent years, the battle ensues in any sphere, public or private, inhabited by women and men, girls and boys. The significance of feminist movement (when it is not co-opted by opportunistic, reactionary forces) is that it offers a new ideological meeting ground for the sexes, a space for criticism, struggle, and transformation. Feminist movement can end the war between the sexes. It can transform relationships so that the alienation, competition, and dehumanization that characterize human interaction can be replaced with feelings of intimacy, mutuality, and camaraderie.

Ironically, these positive implications of feminist movement were often ignored by liberal organizers and participants. Since vocal bourgeois white women were insisting that women repudiate the role of servant to others, they were not interested in convincing men or even other women that feminist movement was important for everyone. Narcissistically, they focused solely on the primacy of feminism in their lives, universalizing their own experiences. Building a mass-based women's movement was never the central issue on their agenda. After many organizations were established, leaders expressed a desire for greater participant diversity; they wanted women to join who were not white, materially privileged, middle-class, or college-educated. It was never deemed necessary for feminist activists to explain to masses of women the significance of feminist movement. Believing their emphasis on social equality was a universal concern, they assumed the idea would carry its own appeal. Strategically, the failure to emphasize the necessity for mass-based movement, grassroots organizing, and sharing with everyone the positive significance of feminist movement helped marginalize feminism by making it appear relevant only to those women who joined organizations.

Recent critiques of feminist movement highlight these failures without stressing the need for revision in strategy and focus. Although the theory and praxis of contemporary feminism with all its

flaws and inadequacies has become well established, even institutionalized, we must try and change its direction if we are to build a
feminist movement that is truly a struggle to end sexist oppression.
In the interest of such a struggle we must, at the onset of our analysis, call attention to the positive, transformative impact the eradication of sexist oppression could have on all our lives.

Many contemporary feminist activists argue that eradicating
sexist oppression is important because it is the primary contradiction, the basis of all other oppressions. Racism, as well as class structure, is perceived as stemming from sexism. Implicit in this line of
analysis is the assumption that the eradication of sexism, "the oldest
oppression," "the primary contradiction," is necessary before attention can be focused on racism or classism. Suggesting a hierarchy of
oppression exists, with sexism in first place, evokes a sense of competing concerns that is unnecessary. While we know that sex-role divisions existed in the earliest civilizations, not enough is known
about these societies to conclusively document the assertion that
women were exploited or oppressed. The earliest civilizations discovered so far have been in archaic black Africa, where presumably
there was no race problem and no class society as we know it today.
The sexism, racism, and classism that exist in the West may resem-
ble systems of domination globally, but they are forms of oppression that have been primarily informed by Western philosophy.
They can be best understood within a Western context, not via an
evolutionary model of human development. Within our society, all
forms of oppression are supported by traditional Western thinking.
The primary contradiction in Western cultural thought is the belief
that the superior should control the inferior. In *The Cultural Basis of
Racism and Group Oppression,* philosopher John Hodge argues that
Western religious and philosophical thought are the ideological basis of all forms of oppression in the United States.

Sexist oppression is of primary importance not because it is the
basis of all other oppression, but because it is the practice of domination most people experience, whether their role be that of
discriminator or discriminated against, exploiter or exploited. It is
the practice of domination most people are socialized to accept be-

fore they even know that other forms of group oppression exist. This does not mean that eradicating sexist oppression would eliminate other forms of oppression. Since all forms of oppression are linked in our society because they are supported by similar institutional and social structures, one system cannot be eradicated while the others remain intact. Challenging sexist oppression is a crucial step in the struggle to eliminate all forms of oppression.

Unlike other forms of oppression, most people witness and/or experience the practice of sexist domination in family settings. We tend to witness and/or experience racism or classism as we encounter the larger society, the world outside the home. In his essay "Dualist Culture and Beyond," Hodge stresses that the family in our society, both traditionally and legally, "reflects the Dualist values of hierarchy and coercive authoritarian control," which are exemplified in parent-child and husband-wife relationships:

> It is in this form of the family where most children first learn the meaning and practice of hierarchical, authoritarian rule. Here is where they learn to accept group oppression against themselves as non-adults, and where they learn to accept male supremacy and the group oppression of women. Here is where they learn that it is the male's role to work in the community and control the economic life of the family and to mete out the physical and financial punishments and rewards, and the female's role to provide the emotional warmth associated with motherhood while under the economic rule of the male. Here is where the relationship of superordination-subordination, of superior-inferior, of master-slave is first learned and accepted as "natural."

Even in families where no male is present, children may learn to value dominating, authoritative rule via their relationship to mothers and other adults, as well as strict adherence to sexist-defined role patterns.

In most societies, family is an important kinship structure: a common ground for people who are linked by blood ties, heredity, or emotive bonds; an environment of care and affirmation, especially for the very young and the very old, who may be unable to care for themselves; a space for communal sharing of resources. In our

society, sexist oppression perverts and distorts the positive function
of family. Family exists as a space wherein we are socialized from
birth to accept and support forms of oppression. In his discussion
of the cultural basis of domination, Hodge emphasizes the role of
the family:

> The traditional Western family, with its authoritarian male rule and
> its authoritarian adult rule, is the major training ground which ini-
> tially conditions us to accept group oppression as the natural order.

Even as we are loved and cared for in families, we are simultaneously taught that this love is not as important as having power to
dominate others. Power struggles, coercive authoritarian rule, and
brutal assertion of domination shape family life so that it is often the
setting of intense suffering and pain. Naturally, individuals flee the
family. Naturally, the family disintegrates.

Contemporary feminist analyses of family often implied that
successful feminist movement would either begin with or lead to the
abolition of family. This suggestion was terribly threatening to many
women, especially non-white women. (In their essay "Challenging
Imperial Feminism," Valerie Amos and Pratibha Parmar examine
the way in which Euro-American feminist discussions of family are
ethnocentric and alienate black women from feminist movement.)
While there are white women activists who may experience family
primarily as an oppressive institution (it may be the social structure
wherein they have experienced grave abuse and exploitation), many
black women find the family the least oppressive institution. Despite sexism in the context of family, we may experience dignity,
self-worth, and a humanization that is not experienced in the outside world wherein we confront all forms of oppression. We know
from our lived experiences that families are not just households
composed of husband, wife, and children, or even blood relations;
we also know that destructive patterns generated by belief in sexism
abound in varied family structures. We wish to affirm the primacy of
family life because we know that family ties are the only sustained
support system for exploited and oppressed peoples. We wish to rid
family life of the abusive dimensions created by sexist oppression

without devaluing it.

Devaluation of family life in feminist discussion often reflects the class nature of the movement. Individuals from privileged classes rely on a number of institutional and social structures to affirm and protect their interests. The bourgeois woman can repudiate family without believing that by so doing she relinquishes the possibility of relationship, care, protection. If all else fails, she can buy care. Since many bourgeois women active in feminist movement were raised in the modern nuclear household, they were particularly subjected to the perversion of family life created by sexist oppression; they may have had material privilege and no experience of abiding family love and care. Their devaluation of family life alienated many women from feminist movement. Ironically, feminism is the one radical political movement that focuses on transforming family relationships. Feminist movement to end sexist oppression affirms family life by its insistence that the purpose of family structure is not to reinforce patterns of domination in the interest of the state. By challenging Western philosophical beliefs that impress on our consciousness a concept of family life that is essentially destructive, feminism would liberate family so that it could be an affirming, positive kinship structure with no oppressive dimensions based on sex differentiation, sexual preference, etc.

Politically, the white supremacist, patriarchal state relies on the family to indoctrinate its members with values supportive of hierarchical control and coercive authority. Therefore, the state has a vested interest in projecting the notion that feminist movement will destroy family life. Introducing a collection of essays, *Rethinking the Family: Some Feminist Questions,* sociologist Barrie Thorne makes the point that feminist critique of family life has been seized upon by New Right groups in their political campaigns:

> Of all the issues raised by feminists, those that bear on the family—among them, demands for abortion rights, and for legitimating an array of household and sexual arrangements, and challenges to men's authority, and women's economic dependence and exclusive responsibility for nurturing—have been the most controversial.

Feminist positions on the family that devalue its importance have been easily co-opted to serve the interests of the state. People are concerned that families are breaking down, that positive dimensions of family life are overshadowed by the aggression, humiliation, abuse, and violence that characterizes the interaction of family members. They must not be convinced that anti-feminism is the way to improve family life. Feminist activists need to affirm the importance of family as a kinship structure that can sustain and nourish people; to graphically address links between sexist oppression and family disintegration; and to give examples, both actual and visionary, of the way family life is and can be when unjust authoritarian rule is replaced with an ethic of communalism, shared responsibility, and mutuality. The movement to end sexist oppression is the only social-change movement that will strengthen and sustain family life in all households.

Within the present family structure, individuals learn to accept sexist oppression as "natural" and are primed to support other forms of oppression, including heterosexist domination. According to Hodge:

> The domination usually present within the family—of children by adults, and of female by male—are forms of group oppression which are easily translated into the "rightful" group oppression of other people defined by "race" (racism), by nationality (colonialism), by "religion," or by "other means."

Significantly, struggle to end sexist oppression that focuses on destroying the cultural basis for such domination strengthens other liberation struggles. Individuals who fight for the eradication of sexism without supporting struggles to end racism or classism undermine their own efforts. Individuals who fight for the eradication of racism or classism while supporting sexist oppression are helping to maintain the cultural basis of all forms of group oppression. While they may initiate successful reforms, their efforts will not lead to revolutionary change. Their ambivalent relationship to oppression in general is a contradiction that must be resolved, or they will daily undermine their own radical work.

Unfortunately, it is not merely the politically naive who demonstrate a lack of awareness that forms of oppression are interrelated. Often brilliant political thinkers have had such blind spots. Men like Frantz Fanon, Albert Memmi, Paulo Freire, and Aimé Césaire, whose works teach us much about the nature of colonization, racism, classism, and revolutionary struggle, often ignore issues of sexist oppression in their own writing. They speak against oppression but then define liberation in terms that suggest it is only oppressed "men" who need freedom. Frantz Fanon's important work *Black Skin, White Masks* draws a portrait of oppression in the first chapter that equates the colonizer with white men and the colonized with black men. Towards the end of the book, Fanon writes of the struggle to overcome alienation:

> The problem considered here is one of time. Those Negroes and white men will be disalienated who refuse to let themselves be sealed away in the materialized Tower of the Past. For many other Negroes, in other ways, disalienation will come into being through their refusal to accept the present definitive.
>
> I am a man, and what I have to recapture is the whole past of the world. I am not responsible solely for the revolt in Santo Domingo.
>
> Every time a man has contributed to the victory of the dignity of the spirit, every time a man has said no to an attempt to subjugate his fellows, I have felt solidarity with his act.

In Paulo Freire's book *Pedagogy of the Oppressed,* a text that has helped many of us to develop political consciousness, there is a tendency to speak of people's liberation as male liberation:

> Liberation is thus a childbirth, and a painful one. The man who emerges is a new man, viable only as the oppressor-oppressed contradiction is superseded by the humanization of all men. Or to put it another way, the solution of this contradiction is borne in the labor which brings into the world this new man: no longer oppressor, no longer oppressed, but man in the process of achieving freedom.

(In a discussion with Freire on this issue, he supported wholeheartedly this criticism of his work and urged me to share this with readers.) The sexist language in these translated texts does not prevent feminist activists from identifying with or learning from the message content. It diminishes without negating the value of the works. It also does support and perpetuate sexist oppression.

Support of sexist oppression in much political writing concerned with revolutionary struggle as well as in the actions of men who advocate revolutionary politics undermines all liberation struggle. In many countries wherein people are engaged in liberation struggle, subordination of women by men is abandoned as the crisis situation compels men to accept and acknowledge women as comrades in struggle, e.g., Cuba, Angola, and Nicaragua. Often when the crisis period has passed, old sexist patterns emerge, antagonism develops, and political solidarity is weakened. It would strengthen and affirm the praxis of any liberation struggle if a commitment to eradicating sexist oppression were a foundation principle shaping all political work. Feminist movement should be of primary significance for all groups and individuals who desire an end to oppression. Many women who would like to participate fully in liberation struggles (the fight against imperialism, racism, classism) are drained of their energies because they are continually confronting and coping with sexist discrimination, exploitation, and oppression. In the interest of continued struggle, solidarity, and sincere commitment to eradicating all forms of domination, sexist oppression cannot continue to be ignored and dismissed by radical political activists.

An important stage in the development of political consciousness is reached when individuals recognize the need to struggle against all forms of oppression. The fight against sexist oppression is of grave political significance—it is not for women only. Feminist movement is vital both in its power to liberate us from the terrible bonds of sexist oppression and in its potential to radicalize and renew other liberation struggles.

4

SISTERHOOD
Political Solidarity
Among Women

Women are the group most victimized by sexist oppression. As with other forms of group oppression, sexism is perpetuated by institutional and social structures; by the individuals who dominate, exploit, or oppress; and by the victims themselves who are socialized to behave in ways that make them act in complicity with the status quo. Male supremacist ideology encourages women to believe we are valueless and obtain value only by relating to or bonding with men. We are taught that our relationships with one another diminish rather than enrich our experience. We are taught that women are "natural" enemies, that solidarity will never exist between us because we cannot, should not, and do not bond with one another. We have learned these lessons well. We must unlearn them if we are to build a sustained feminist movement. We must learn to live and work in solidarity. We must learn the true meaning and value of Sisterhood.

Although contemporary feminist movement should have provided a training ground for women to learn about political solidarity, Sisterhood was not viewed as a revolutionary accomplishment women would work and struggle to obtain. The vision of Sisterhood evoked by women's liberationists was based on the idea of common oppression. Needless to say, it was primarily bourgeois white women, both liberal and radical in perspective, who professed belief in the notion of "common oppression." The idea of common oppression was a false and corrupt platform disguising and mystifying the true nature of women's varied and complex social reality. Women are divided by sexist attitudes, racism, class privilege, and a host of other prejudices. Sustained woman bonding can occur only when these divisions are confronted and the necessary steps are taken to eliminate them. Divisions will not be eliminated by wishful thinking or romantic reverie about common oppression despite the value of highlighting experiences all women share.

In recent years, Sisterhood as slogan, motto, rallying cry no longer evokes the spirit of power in unity. Some feminists now seem to feel that unity among women is impossible given our differences. Abandoning the idea of Sisterhood as an expression of political solidarity weakens and diminishes feminist movement. Solidarity strengthens resistance struggle. There can be no mass-based feminist movement to end sexist oppression without a united front—women must take the initiative and demonstrate the power of solidarity. Unless we can show that barriers separating women can be eliminated, that solidarity can exist, we cannot hope to change and transform society as a whole. The shift away from an emphasis on Sisterhood has occurred because many women—angered by the insistence on common oppression, shared identity, sameness—criticized or dismissed feminist movement altogether. The emphasis on Sisterhood was often seen as the emotional appeal masking the opportunism of manipulative bourgeois white women. It was seen as a cover-up hiding the fact that many women exploit and oppress other women. Black woman activist lawyer Florynce Kennedy wrote an essay in the anthology *Sisterhood Is Powerful* voicing her suspicions about the existence of solidarity among women as early as 1970:

> It is for this reason that I have considerable difficulty with the sisterhood mystique: "We are sisters," "Don't criticize a 'sister' publicly," etc. When a female judge asks my client where the bruises are when she complains about being assaulted by her husband (as did Family Court Judge Sylvia Jaffin Liese), and makes smart remarks about her being overweight, and when another female judge is so hostile that she disqualifies herself but refuses to order a combative husband out of the house (even though he owns

property elsewhere with suitable living quarters)—these judges are not my sisters.

Women were wise to reject a false Sisterhood based on shallow notions of bonding. We are mistaken if we allow these distortions or the women who created them (many of whom now tell us bonding between women is unimportant) to lead us to devalue Sisterhood. (In early contemporary feminist writings (e.g., the "Redstockings Manifesto") the image of woman as victim was evoked. Joan Cassell's study of sisterhood and symbolism in the feminist movement, *A Group Called Women,* examines the ideology of bonding among feminist activists. Contemporary writers like Leah Fritz evoke an image of woman as victim to encourage woman bonding. Barbara Smith discusses this tendency in her introduction to *Home Girls.*)

Women are enriched when we bond with one another, but we cannot develop sustaining ties or political solidarity using the model of Sisterhood created by bourgeois women's liberationists. According to their analysis, the basis for bonding was shared victimization, hence the emphasis on common oppression. This concept of bonding directly reflects male supremacist thinking. Sexist ideology teaches women that to be female is to be a victim. Rather than repudiate this equation (which mystifies female experience—in their daily lives most women are not continually passive, helpless, or powerless "victims"), women's liberationists embraced it, making shared victimization the basis for woman bonding. This meant that women had to conceive of themselves as "victims" in order to feel that feminist movement was relevant to their lives. Bonding as victims created a situation in which assertive, self-affirming women were often seen as having no place in feminist movement. It was this logic that led white women activists (along with black men) to suggest that black women were so "strong" they did not need to be active in feminist movement. It was this logic that led many white women activists to abandon feminist movement when they no longer embraced the victim identity. Ironically, the women who were most eager to be seen as "victims," who overwhelmingly stressed

the role of victim, were more privileged and powerful than the vast
majority of women in our society. An example of this tendency is
some writing about violence against women. Women who are exploited and oppressed daily cannot afford to relinquish the belief
that they exercise some measure of control, however relative, over
their lives. They cannot afford to see themselves solely as "victims"
because their survival depends on continued exercise of whatever
personal powers they possess. It would be psychologically demoral-
izing for these women to bond with other women on the basis of
shared victimization. They bond with other women on the basis of
shared strengths and resources. This is the woman bonding feminist
movement should encourage. It is this type of bonding that is the essence of Sisterhood.

Bonding as "victims," white women liberationists were not re-
quired to assume responsibility for confronting the complexity of
their own experience. They were not challenging one another to examine their sexist attitudes towards women unlike themselves or exploring the impact of race and class privilege on their relationships
to women outside their race/class groups. Identifying as "victims,"
they could abdicate responsibility for their role in the maintenance
and perpetuation of sexism, racism, and classism, which they did by
insisting that only men were the enemy. They did not acknowledge
and confront the enemy within. They were not prepared to forego
privilege and do the "dirty work" (the struggle and confrontation
necessary to build political awareness, as well as the many tedious
tasks to be accomplished in day-to-day organizing) that is necessary
in the development of radical political consciousness, the first task
being honest critique and evaluation of one's social status, values,
political beliefs, etc. Sisterhood became yet another shield against
reality, another support system. Their version of Sisterhood was informed by racist and classist assumptions about white womanhood,
that the white "lady" (that is to say bourgeois woman) should be
protected from all that might upset or discomfort her and shielded
from negative realities that might lead to confrontation. Their version of Sisterhood dictated that sisters were to "unconditionally"
love one another; that they were to avoid conflict and minimize dis-

agreement; that they were not to criticize one other, especially in public. For a time these mandates created an illusion of unity, suppressing the competition, hostility, perpetual disagreement, and abusive criticism (trashing) that was often the norm in feminist groups. Today many splinter groups who share common identities (e.g., the WASP working class, white academic faculty women, anarchist feminists, etc.) use this same model of Sisterhood, but participants in these groups endeavor to support, affirm, and protect one another while demonstrating hostility (usually through excessive trashing) towards women outside the chosen sphere. Bonding among a chosen circle of women who strengthen their ties by excluding and devaluing women outside their group closely resembles the type of personal bonding among women that has always occurred under patriarchy—the one difference being the interest in feminism.

At the onset of contemporary feminist movement, I (and many other black women) often heard white women in women's studies classes, consciousness-raising groups, meetings, etc. respond to questions about the lack of black female participation by stressing that this was not related to problems with the structure of feminist movement but an indication that black women were already liberated. The image of the "strong" black woman is evoked in the writings of a number of white activists (e.g., Sara Evans, *Personal Politics;* Bettina Aptheker, *Woman's Legacy*).

To develop political solidarity among women, feminist activists cannot bond on the terms set by the dominant ideology of the culture. We must define our own terms. Rather than bond on the basis of shared victimization or in response to a false sense of a common enemy, we can bond on the basis of our political commitment to a feminist movement that aims to end sexist oppression. Given such a commitment, our energies would not be concentrated on the issue of equality with men or solely on the struggle to resist male domination. We would no longer accept a simplistic good girls/bad boys account of the structure of sexist oppression. Before we can resist male domination we must break our attachment to sexism; we must work to transform female consciousness. Working together to expose, examine, and eliminate sexist socialization within ourselves,

women would strengthen and affirm one another and build a solid
foundation for developing political solidarity.

Between women and men, sexism is most often expressed in
the form of male domination, which leads to discrimination, exploitation, or oppression. Between women, male supremacist values are
expressed through suspicious, defensive, competitive behavior. It is
sexism that leads women to feel threatened by one another without
cause. While sexism teaches women to be sex objects for men, it is
also manifest when women who have repudiated this role feel con-
temptuous and superior in relation to those women who have not.
Sexism leads women to devalue parenting work while inflating the
value of jobs and careers. Acceptance of sexist ideology is indicated
when women teach children that there are only two possible behavior patterns: the role of dominant or submissive being. Sexism
teaches women woman-hating, and both consciously and unconsciously we act out this hatred in our daily contact with one another.

Although contemporary feminist activists, especially radical
feminists, called attention to women's absorption in sexist ideology,
ways that women who are advocates of patriarchy, as well as women
who uncritically accept sexist assumptions, could unlearn that socialization were not stressed. It was often assumed that to support
feminism was synonymous with repudiation of sexism in all its
forms. Taking on the label "feminist" was accepted as a sign of personal transformation; as a consequence, the process by which values
were altered was either ignored or could not be spelled out because
no fundamental change had occurred. Sometimes consciousness-raising groups provided space for women to explore their sexism. This examination of attitudes towards themselves and other
women was often a catalyst for transformation. Describing the
function of rap groups in *The Politics of Women's Liberation,* Jo Freeman explains:

> Women came together in small groups to share personal experi-
> ences, problems, and feelings. From this public sharing comes
> the realization that what was thought to be individual is in fact
> common: that what was thought to be a personal problem has a

social cause and a political solution. The rap group attacks the effects of psychological oppression and helps women to put it into a feminist context. Women learn to see how social structures and attitudes have molded them from birth and limited their opportunities. They ascertain the extent to which women have been denigrated in this society and how they have developed prejudices against themselves and other women. They learn to develop self-esteem and to appreciate the value of group solidarity.

As consciousness-raising groups lost their popularity, new groups were not formed to fulfill similar functions. Women produced a large quantity of feminist writing but placed little emphasis on ways to unlearn sexism.

Since we live in a society that promotes fads and temporary superficial adaptation of different values, we are easily convinced that changes have occurred in arenas where there has been little or no change. Women's sexist attitudes towards one another are one such arena. All over the United States, women spend hours of their time daily verbally abusing other women, usually through malicious gossip (not to be confused with gossip as positive communication). Television soap operas and night-time dramas continually portray woman-to-woman relationships as characterized by aggression, contempt, and competitiveness. In feminist circles, sexism towards women is expressed by abusive trashing, and total disregard and lack of concern or interest in women who have not joined feminist movement. This is especially evident at university campuses where feminist studies is often seen as a discipline or program having no relationship to feminist movement. In her commencement address at Barnard College in May 1979, black woman writer Toni Morrison told her audience:

> I want not to ask you but to tell you not to participate in the oppression of your sisters. Mothers who abuse their children are women, and another woman, not an agency, has to be willing to stay their hands. Mothers who set fire to school buses are women, and another woman, not an agency, has to tell them to stay their hands. Women who stop the promotion of other women in careers are women, and another woman must come to the victim's

aid. Social and welfare workers who humiliate their clients may be women, and other women colleagues have to deflect their anger.

I am alarmed by the violence that women do to each other: professional violence, competitive violence, emotional violence. I am alarmed by the willingness of women to enslave other women. I am alarmed by a growing absence of decency on the killing floor of professional women's worlds.

To build a politicized, mass-based feminist movement, women must work harder to overcome the alienation from one another that exists when sexist socialization has not been unlearned, e.g., homophobia, judging by appearance, conflicts between women with diverse sexual practices. So far, feminist movement has not transformed woman-to-woman relationships, especially between women who are strangers to one another or from different backgrounds, even though it has been the occasion for bonding between individuals and groups of women. We must renew our efforts to help women unlearn sexism if we are to develop affirming personal relationships as well as political unity.

Racism is another barrier to solidarity between women. The ideology of Sisterhood as expressed by contemporary feminist activists indicated no acknowledgment that racist discrimination, exploitation, and oppression of multi-ethnic women by white women had made it impossible for the two groups to feel they shared common interests or political concerns. Also, the existence of totally different cultural backgrounds can make communication difficult. This has been especially true of black and white female relationships. Historically, many black women experienced white women as the white supremacist group who most directly exercised power over them, often in a manner far more brutal and dehumanizing than that of racist white men. Today, despite predominant rule by white supremacist patriarchs, black women often work in situations where their immediate supervisor, boss, or authority figure is a white woman. Conscious of the privileges white men as well as white women gain as a consequence of racial domination, black women were quick to react to the feminist call for Sisterhood by pointing to the contradiction—that we should join with women who exploit us to help liberate them. The call for Sisterhood was heard by many black women as a plea for help and support for a movement that did not address us. As Toni Morrison explains in her article "What the Black Woman Thinks about Women's Lib," many black women do not respect bourgeois white women and could not imagine supporting a cause that would be for their benefit:

> Black women have been able to envy white women (their looks, their easy life, the attention they seem to get from their men); they could fear them (for the economic control they have had over black women's lives); and even love them (as mammies and domestic workers can); but black women have found it impossible to respect white women.... Black women have no abiding admiration of white women as competent, complete people, whether vying with them for the few professional slots available to women in general, or moving their dirt from one place to another, they regarded them as willful children, pretty children, mean children, but never as real adults capable of handling the real problems of the world.
>
> White women were ignorant of the facts of life—perhaps by choice, perhaps with the assistance of men, but ignorant anyway. They were totally dependent on marriage or male support (emotionally and economically). They confronted their sexuality with furtiveness, complete abandon, or repression. Those who could afford it gave over the management of the house and the rearing of children to others. (It is a source of amusement even now to black women to listen to feminist talk of liberation while somebody's nice black grandmother shoulders the daily responsibility of child-rearing and floor-mopping, and the liberated one comes home to examine the housekeeping, correct it, and be entertained by the children.) If Women's Lib needs those grandmothers to thrive, it has a serious flaw.

Many perceived that women's liberation movement as outlined by bourgeois white women would serve their interests at the expense of poor and working-class women, many of whom are black. Certainly this was not a basis for Sisterhood, and black women would have been politically naive had we joined such a movement. However, given the struggles of black women's participation historically and

currently in political organizing, the emphasis could have been on
the development and clarification of the nature of political solidarity.

White females discriminate against and exploit black women
while simultaneously being envious and competitive in their interactions with them. Neither process of interaction creates conditions
wherein trust and mutually reciprocal relationships can develop. After constructing feminist theory and praxis in such a way as to omit
focus on racism, white women shifted the responsibility for calling
attention to race onto others. They did not have to take the initiative
in discussions of racism or race privilege but could listen and respond to non-white women discussing racism without changing in
any way the structure of feminist movement, without losing their
hegemonic hold. They could then show their concern with having
more women of color in feminist organizations by encouraging
greater participation. They were not confronting racism. In more recent years, racism has become an accepted topic in feminist discussions not as a result of black women calling attention to it (this was
done at the very onset of the movement), but as a result of white female input validating such discussions, a process which is indicative
of how racism works. Commenting on this tendency in her essay
"The Incompatible Ménage à Trois: Marxism, Feminism, and Racism," Gloria Joseph states:

> To date feminists have not concretely demonstrated the potential
> or capacity to become involved in fighting racism on an equal
> footing with sexism. Adrienne Rich's recent article on feminism
> and racism is an exemplary one on this topic. She reiterates much
> that has been voiced by black female writers, but the acclaim
> given her article shows again that it takes whiteness to give even
> Blackness validity.

Focus on racism in feminist circles is usually directed at legiti-
mating the "as is" structure of feminist theory and praxis. Like other
affirmative-action agendas in white supremacist, capitalist patriarchy, lengthy discussions of racism or lip service to its importance
tend to call attention to the "political correctness" of current feminist movement; they are not directed at an overall struggle to resist

racist oppression in our society (not just racism in feminist movement). Discussions of racism have been implicitly sexist because of
the focus on guilt and personal behavior. Racism is not an issue simply because white women activists are individually racist. They represent a small percentage of women in this society. They could have
all been anti-racist from the outset, but eliminating racism would
still need to be a central feminist issue. Racism is fundamentally a
feminist issue because it is so interconnected with sexist oppression.
In the West, the philosophical foundations of racist and sexist ideology are similar. Although ethnocentric white values have led feminist theorists to argue the priority of sexism over racism, they do so
in the context of attempting to create an evolutionary notion of culture, which in no way corresponds to our lived experience. In the
United States, maintaining white supremacy has always been as great
if not a greater priority than maintaining strict sex-role divisions. It is
no mere coincidence that interest in white women's rights is kindled
whenever there is mass-based, anti-racist protest. Even the most politically naive person can comprehend that a white supremacist state,
asked to respond to the needs of oppressed black people and/or the
needs of white women (particularly those from the bourgeois
classes), will find it in its interest to respond to whites. Radical
movement to end racism (a struggle that many have died to advance) is far more threatening than a women's movement shaped to
meet the class needs of upwardly mobile white women.

It does not in any way diminish the value of or the need for feminist movement to recognize the significance of anti-racist struggle.
Feminist theory would have much to offer if it showed women ways
in which racism and sexism are immutably connected, rather than
pitting one struggle against the other or blatantly dismissing racism.
A central issue for feminist activists has been the struggle to obtain
for women the right to control their bodies. The very concept of
white supremacy relies on the perpetuation of a white race. It is in
the interest of continued white racist domination of the planet for
white patriarchy to maintain control over all women's bodies. Any
white female activist who works daily to help women gain control
over their bodies and is racist negates and undermines her own ef-

fort. When white women attack white supremacy they are simultaneously participating in the struggle to end sexist oppression. This is
just one example of the intersecting, complementary nature of racist
and sexist oppression. There are many others that need to be examined by feminist theorists.

Racism allows white women to construct feminist theory and
praxis in such a way that it is far removed from anything resembling
radical struggle. Racist socialization teaches bourgeois white women
to think they are necessarily more capable of leading masses of
women than other groups of women. Time and time again, they
have shown that they do not want to be part of feminist movement—they want to lead it. Even though bourgeois white women
liberationists probably know less about grassroots organizing than
many poor and working-class women, they were certain of their
leadership ability, as well as confident that theirs should be the dominant role in shaping theory and praxis. Racism teaches an inflated
sense of importance and value, especially when coupled with class
privilege. Most poor and working-class women, or even individual,
bourgeois, non-white women, would not have assumed that they
could launch a feminist movement without first having the support
and participation of diverse groups of women. Elizabeth Spelman
stresses this impact of racism in her essay "Theories of Race and
Gender: The Erasure of Black Women":

> This is a racist society, and part of what this means is that, gener-
> ally, the self-esteem of white people is deeply influenced by their
> difference from and supposed superiority to black people. White
> people may not think of themselves as racists, because they do
> not own slaves or hate blacks, but that does not mean that much
> of what props up white people's sense of self-esteem is not based
> on the racism which unfairly distributes benefits and burdens to
> whites and blacks.

One reason white women active in feminist movement were unwilling to confront racism was their arrogant assumption that their call
for Sisterhood was a non-racist gesture. Many white women have
said to me, "We wanted black women and other non-white women

to join the movement," totally unaware of their perception that they somehow "own" the movement, that they are the "hosts" inviting us as "guests."

Despite current focus on eliminating racism in feminist movement, there has been little change in the direction of theory and praxis. While white feminist activists now include writings by women of color on course outlines, or hire one woman of color to teach a class about her ethnic group, or make sure one or more women of color are represented in feminist organizations (even though this contribution of women of color is needed and valuable), more often than not they are attempting to cover up the fact that they are totally unwilling to surrender their hegemonic dominance of theory and praxis, a dominance which they would not have established were this not a white supremacist, capitalist state. Their attempts to manipulate women of color, a component of the process of dehumanization, do not always go unnoticed. In the July 1983 issue of *In These Times,* a letter written by Theresa Funiciello was published on the subject of poor women and the women's movement that shows the nature of racism within feminist movement:

> Prior to a conference some time ago on the Urban Woman sponsored by the New York City chapter of NOW, I received a phone call from a NOW representative (whose name I have forgotten) asking for a welfare speaker with special qualifications. I was asked that she not be white—she might be "too articulate"—(i.e., not me), that she not be black, she might be "too angry." Perhaps she could be Puerto Rican? She should not say anything political or analytical but confine herself to the subject of "what the women's movement has done for me."

Funiciello responded to this situation by organizing a multi-racial women's takeover of the conference. This type of action shows the spirit of Sisterhood.

Another response to racism has been the establishment of unlearning racism workshops, which are often led by white women. These workshops are important, yet they tend to focus primarily on cathartic, individual psychological acknowledgment of personal prejudice without stressing the need for corresponding change in political commitment and action. A woman who attends an unlearning racism workshop and learns to acknowledge that she is racist is no less a threat than one who does not. Acknowledgment of racism is significant when it leads to transformation. More research, writing, and practical implementation of findings must be done on ways to unlearn racist socialization. Many white women who daily exercise race privilege lack awareness that they are doing so (which explains the emphasis on confession in unlearning racism workshops). They may not have conscious understanding of the ideology of white supremacy and the extent to which it shapes their behavior and attitudes towards women unlike themselves. Often, white women bond on the basis of shared racial identity without conscious awareness of the significance of their actions. This unconscious maintenance and perpetuation of white supremacy is dangerous, because none of us can struggle to change racist attitudes if we do not recognize that they exist. For example, a group of white feminist activists who do not know one another may be present at a meeting to discuss feminist theory. They may feel they are bonded on the basis of shared womanhood, but the atmosphere will noticeably change when a woman of color enters the room. The white women will become tense, no longer relaxed, no longer celebratory. Unconsciously, they feel close to one another because they shared racial identity. The "whiteness" that bonds them together is a racial identity that is directly related to the experience of non-white people as "other" and as a "threat." Often when I speak to white women about racial bonding, they deny that it exists; it is not unlike sexist men denying their sexism. Until white supremacy is understood and attacked by white women, there can be no bonding between them and multi-ethnic groups of women.

Women will know that white feminist activists have begun to confront racism in a serious and revolutionary manner when they are not simply acknowledging racism in feminist movement or calling attention to personal prejudice, but are actively struggling to resist racist oppression in our society. Women will know they have made a political commitment to eliminating racism when they help change the direction of feminist movement, when they work to un-learn racist socialization prior to assuming positions of leadership or shaping theory or making contact with women "of color" so that they will not perpetuate and maintain racial oppression or, unconsciously or consciously, abuse and hurt non-white women. These are the truly radical gestures that create a foundation for the experience of political solidarity between white women and women of color.

White women are not the only group who must confront racism if Sisterhood is to emerge. Women of color must confront our absorption of white supremacist beliefs, "internalized racism," which may lead us to feel self-hate, to vent anger and rage at injustice at one another rather than at oppressive forces, to hurt and abuse one another, or to lead one ethnic group to make no effort to communicate with another. Often women of color from varied ethnic groups have learned to resent and hate one another, or to be competitive with one another. Often Asian, Latina, or Native American Indian groups find they can bond with whites by hating blacks. Black people respond to this by perpetuating racist stereotypes and images of these ethnic groups. It becomes a vicious cycle. Divisions between women of color will not be eliminated until we assume responsibility for uniting (not solely on the basis of resisting racism) to learn about our cultures, to share our knowledge and skills, and to gain strength from our diversity. We need to do more research and writing about the barriers that separate us and the ways we can overcome such separation. Often the men in our ethnic groups have greater contact with one another than we do. Women often assume so many job-related and domestic responsibilities that we lack the time or do not make the time to get to know women outside our group or community. Language differences often prevent us from communicating; we can change this by encouraging one another to learn to speak Spanish, English, Japanese, Chinese, etc.

One factor that makes interaction between multi-ethnic groups of women difficult and sometimes impossible is our failure to recognize that a behavior pattern in one culture may be unacceptable in another, that it may have different signification cross-culturally. Through repeated teaching of a course titled "Third World Women in the United States," I have learned the importance of learning what we called one another's cultural codes. An Asian American student of Japanese heritage explained her reluctance to participate in feminist organizations by calling attention to the tendency among feminist activists to speak rapidly without pause, to be quick on the uptake, always ready with a response. She had been raised to pause and think before speaking, to consider the impact of one's words, a characteristic that she felt was particularly true of Asian Americans. She expressed feelings of inadequacy on the various occasions she was present in feminist groups. In our class, we learned to allow pauses and appreciate them. By sharing this cultural code, we created an atmosphere in the classroom that allowed for different communication patterns. This particular class was peopled primarily by black women. Several white women students complained that the atmosphere in the class was "too hostile." They cited the noise level and direct confrontations that took place in the room prior to class as an example of this hostility. Our response was to explain that what they perceived as hostility and aggression, we considered playful teasing and affectionate expressions of our pleasure at being together. Our tendency to talk loudly we saw as a consequence of being in a room with many people speaking, as well as of cultural background: many of us were raised in families where individuals speak loudly. In their upbringing as white, middle-class females, the complaining students had been taught to identify loud and direct speech with anger. We explained that we did not identify loud or blunt speech in this way, and encouraged them to switch codes, to think of it as an affirming gesture. Once they switched codes, they not only began to have a more creative, joyful experience in the class, but they also learned that silence and quiet speech can in some cultures indicate hostility and aggression. By learning one another's cultural codes and respecting our differences, we felt a sense of community, of Sisterhood. Respecting diversity does not mean uniformity or sameness. (My experience teaching "Third World Women in the United States" at San Francisco State has deeply enriched my understanding of women from diverse backgrounds. I am grateful to all the students I taught there, especially Betty and Susan.)

A crucial concern in these multi-racial classroom settings was recognition and acknowledgment of our differences and the extent to which they determine how we will be perceived by others. We had to continually remind one another to appreciate difference since many of us were raised to fear it. We talked about the need to acknowledge that we all suffer in some way, but that we are not all oppressed nor equally oppressed. Many of us feared that our experiences were irrelevant because they were not as oppressive or as exploited as the experiences of others. We discovered that we had a greater feeling of unity when people focused truthfully on their own experiences without comparing them with those of others in a competitive way. One student, Isabel Yrigoyei, wrote:

> We are not equally oppressed. There is no joy in this. We must speak from within us, our own experiences, our own oppressions—taking someone else's oppression is nothing to feel proud of. We should never speak for that which we have not felt.

When we began our communication by focusing on individual experiences, we found them to be varied even among those of us who shared common ethnic backgrounds. We learned that these differences mean we have no monolithic experiences that we can identity as "Chicana experience," "Black experience," etc. A Chicana growing up in a rural environment in a Spanish-speaking home has a life experience that differs from that of a Chicana raised in an English-speaking family in a bourgeois, predominantly white New Jersey suburb. These two women will not automatically feel solidarity. Even though they are from the same ethnic group, they must work to develop Sisterhood. Seeing these types of differences, we also confronted our tendency to value some experiences over others. We might see the Spanish-speaking Chicana as being more "politically correct" than her English-speaking peer. By no longer passively accepting the learned tendency to compare and judge, we could see value in each experience. We could also see that our different experiences often meant that we had different needs, that there was no one strategy or formula for the development of political consciousness. By mapping out various strategies, we affirmed our di-

versity while working towards solidarity. Women must explore
various ways to communicate with one another cross-culturally if
we are to develop political solidarity. When women of color strive to
learn with and about one another, we take responsibility for building
Sisterhood. We need not rely on white women to lead the way to solidarity; all too often, opportunistic concerns point them in other directions. We can establish unity among ourselves with anti-racist
women. We can stand together united in political solidarity, in feminist movement. We can restore to the idea of Sisterhood its true
meaning and value.

Cutting across racial lines, class is a serious political division between women. It was often suggested in early feminist literature that
class would not be so important if more poor and working-class
women would join the movement. Such thinking was both a denial
of the existence of class privilege gained through exploitation as well
as a denial of class struggle. To build Sisterhood, women must criticize and repudiate class exploitation. The bourgeois woman who
takes a less privileged "sister" to lunch or dinner at a fancy restau-
rant may be acknowledging class, but she is not repudiating class
privilege—she is exercising it. Wearing second-hand clothing and
living in low-cost housing in a poor neighborhood while buying stock
is not a gesture of solidarity with those who are deprived or underprivileged. As in the case of racism in feminist movement, the emphasis on class has been focused on individual status and change. Until
women accept the need for redistribution of wealth and resources in
the United States and work towards the achievement of that end,
there will be no bonding among women that transcends class.

It is terribly apparent that feminist movement so far has primarily served the class interests of bourgeois white women and men.
The great majority of women from middle-class situations who recently entered the labor force (an entry encouraged and promoted
by feminist movement) helped strengthen the economy of the
1970s. In *The Two-Paycheck Marriage,* Caroline Bird emphasizes the
extent to which these women (most of whom are white) helped bol-
ster a waning economy:

Working wives helped families maintain that standard of living through inflation. The Bureau of Labor Statistics has concluded that between 1973 and 1974 the real purchasing power of single-earner families dropped 3 percent compared with only 1 percent for families in which the wife was working.... Women especially will put themselves out to defend a standard of living they see threatened.

Women did more than maintain standards. Working women lifted millions of families into middle-class life. Her pay meant the difference between an apartment and a house, or college for the children...

Working wives were beginning to create a new kind of rich—and...a new kind of poor.

More than ten years later, it is evident that large numbers of individual white women (especially those from middle-class backgrounds) have made economic strides in the wake of feminist movement support of careerism and affirmative-action programs in many professions. However, the masses of women are as poor as ever, or poorer. To the bourgeois "feminist," the million-dollar salary granted newscaster Barbara Walters represents a victory for women. To working-class women who make less than the minimum wage and receive few, if any, benefits, it means continued class exploitation.

Leah Fritz's *Dreamers and Dealers* is a fine example of the liberal woman's attempt to gloss over the fact that class privilege is based on exploitation; that rich women support and condone that exploitation; that the people who suffer most are poor, underprivileged women and children. Fritz attempts to evoke sympathy for all upper-class women by stressing their psychological suffering, their victimization at the hands of men. She concludes her chapter "Rich Women" with the statement:

Feminism belongs as much to the rich woman as to the poor woman. It can help her to understand that her own interests are linked with the advancement of all womankind; that comfort in dependency is a trap; that the golden cage has bars, too; and that, rich and poor, we are all wounded in the service of the patriarchy, although our scars are different. The inner turmoil that sends her to a psychoanalyst can generate energy for the movement which alone may heal her, by setting her free.

Fritz conveniently ignores that domination and exploitation are necessary if there are to be rich women who may experience sexist discrimination or exploitation. She conveniently ignores class struggle.

Women from lower-class groups had no difficulty recognizing that the social equality women's liberationists talked about equated careerism and class mobility with liberation. They also knew who would be exploited in the service of this liberation. Daily confronting class exploitation, they cannot conveniently ignore class struggle. In the anthology *Women of Crisis,* Helen, a working-class white woman who works as a maid in the home of a bourgeois white "feminist," expresses her understanding of the contradiction between feminist rhetoric and practice:

> I think the missus is right: everyone should be equal. She keeps on saying that. But then she has me working away in her house, and I'm not equal with her—and she doesn't want to be equal with me; and I don't blame her, because if I was her I'd hold on to my money just like she does. Maybe that's what the men are doing—they're holding on to their money. And it's a big fight, like it always is about money. She should know. She doesn't go throwing big fat paychecks at her "help." She's fair; she keeps on reminding us—but she's not going to "liberate" us, any more than the men are going to "liberate" their wives or their secretaries or the other women working in their companies.

Women's liberationists not only equated psychological pain with material deprivation to de-emphasize class privilege; they often suggested it was the more severe problem. They managed to overlook the fact that many women suffer both psychologically and materially, and for that reason alone changing their social status merited greater attention than careerism. Certainly the bourgeois woman who is suffering psychically is more likely to find help than the woman who is suffering material deprivation as well as emotional pain. One of the basic differences in perspective between the bourgeois woman and the working-class or poor woman is that the latter knows that being discriminated against or exploited because one is female may be painful and dehumanizing, but it may not necessarily be as painful, dehumanizing, or threatening as being without food or shelter, as starvation, as being deathly ill but unable to obtain medical care. Had poor women set the agenda for feminist movement, they might have decided that class struggle would be a central feminist issue, that poor and privileged women would work to understand class structure and the way it pits women against one another.

Outspoken socialist feminists, most of whom are white women, have emphasized class, but they have not been effective in changing attitudes towards class in feminist movement. Despite their support of socialism, their values, behaviors, and lifestyles continue to be shaped by privilege. They have not developed collective strategies to convince bourgeois women who have no radical political perspective that eliminating class oppression is crucial to efforts to end sexist oppression. They have not worked hard to organize with poor and working-class women who may not identify as socialists but do identify with the need for redistribution of wealth in the United States. They have not worked to raise the consciousness of women collectively. Much of their energy has been spent addressing the white male left, discussing the connections between Marxism and feminism, or explaining to other feminist activists that socialist feminism is the best strategy for revolution. Emphasis on class struggle is often incorrectly deemed the sole domain of socialist feminists. Although I call attention to directions and strategies they have not employed, I wish to emphasize that these issues should be addressed by all activists in feminist movement. When women face the reality of classism and make political commitments to eliminating it, we will no longer experience the class conflicts that have been so apparent in feminist movement. Until we focus on class divisions among women, we will be unable to build political solidarity.

Sexism, racism, and classism divide women from one another. Within feminist movement, divisions and disagreements about strategy and emphasis led to the formation of a number of groups with varied political positions. Splintering into different political factions and special-interest groups has erected unnecessary barriers to Sisterhood that could easily be eliminated. Special-interest groups lead women to believe that only socialist feminists should be concerned about class; that only lesbian feminists should be concerned about the oppression of lesbians and gay men; that only black women or other women of color should be concerned about racism. Every woman can stand in political opposition to sexist, racist, heterosexist, and classist oppression. While she may choose to focus her work on a given political issue or a particular cause, if she is firmly opposed to all forms of group oppression, this broad perspective will be manifest in all her work irrespective of its particularity. When feminist activists are anti-racist and against class exploitation, it will not matter if women of color or poor women, etc., are present. These issues will be deemed important and will be addressed, although the women most personally affected by particular exploitations will necessarily continue in the forefront of those struggles. Women must learn to accept responsibility for fighting oppressions that may not directly affect us as individuals. Feminist movement, like other radical movements in our society, suffers when individual concerns and priorities are the only reason for participation. When we show our concern for the collective, we strengthen our solidarity.

"Solidarity" was a word seldom used in contemporary feminist movement. Much greater emphasis was placed on the idea of "support." Support can mean upholding or defending a position one believes is right. It can also mean serving as a prop or a foundation for a weak structure. This latter meaning had greater significance in feminist circles. Its value emerged from the emphasis on shared victimization. Identifying as "victims," women were acknowledging a helplessness and powerlessness as well as a need for support, in this case the support of fellow feminist activists, "sisters." It was closely related to the shallow notion of Sisterhood. Commenting on its usage among feminist activists in her essay "With All Due Respect," Jane Rule explains:

> Support is a much used word in the women's movement. For too many people it means giving and receiving unqualified approval. Some women are awfully good at withdrawing it at crucial mo-

ments. Too many are convinced they can't function without it. It's a false concept which has produced barriers to understanding and done real emotional damage. Suspension of critical judgment is not necessary for offering real support, which has to do instead with self-respect and respect for other people even at moments of serious disagreement.

Women's legacy of woman-hating, which includes fierce, brutal, verbal tearing apart of one another, has to be eliminated if women are to make critiques and engage in disagreements and arguments that are constructive and caring, with the intention of enriching rather than diminishing. Woman-to-woman negative, aggressive behavior is not unlearned when all critical judgment is suspended. It is unlearned when women accept that we are different, that we will necessarily disagree, but that we can disagree and argue with one another without acting as if we are fighting for our lives, without feeling that we stand to lose all self-esteem by verbally trashing someone else. Verbal disagreements are often the setting where women can demonstrate their engagement with the win-or-lose competitiveness that is most often associated with male interactions, especially in the arena of sports. Women, like men, must learn how to dialogue with one another without competition. Rule suggests that women can disagree without trashing if they realize they do not stand to lose value or self-worth if they are criticized: "No one can discredit my life if it is in my own hands, and therefore I do not have to make anyone carry the false burden of my frightened hostility."

Women need to come together in situations where there will be ideological disagreement and work to change that interaction so communication occurs. This means that when women come together, rather than pretend union, we would acknowledge that we are divided and must develop strategies to overcome fears, prejudices, resentments, competitiveness, etc. The fierce negative disagreements that have taken place in feminist circles have led many feminist activists to shun group or individual interaction where there is likely to be disagreement which leads to confrontation. Safety and support have been redefined to mean hanging out in groups where the participants are alike and share similar values.

While no woman wants to enter a situation in which she will be psychically annihilated, women can face one another in hostile confrontation and struggle and move beyond the hostility to understanding. Expression of hostility as an end in itself is a useless activity, but when it is the catalyst pushing us on to greater clarity and understanding, it serves a meaningful function.

Women need to have the experience of working through hostility to arrive at understanding and solidarity, if only to free ourselves from the sexist socialization that tells us to avoid confrontation because we will be victimized or destroyed. Time and time again, I have had the experience of making statements at talks that anger a listener and lead to assertive and sometimes hostile verbal confrontation. The situation feels uncomfortable, negative, and unproductive because there are angry voices, tears, etc., and yet I may find later that the experience has led to greater clarity and growth on my part and on the part of the listener. On one occasion, I was invited by a black woman sociologist, a very soft-spoken individual, to speak in a class she was teaching. A young Chicana woman who could pass for white was a student in the class. We had a heated exchange when I made the point that the ability to pass for white gave her a perspective on race totally different from that of someone who is dark-skinned and can never pass. I pointed out that any person meeting her with no knowledge of her ethnic background probably assumes that she is white and relates to her accordingly. At the time the suggestion angered her. She became quite angry and finally stormed out of the class in tears. The teacher and fellow students definitely saw me as the "bad guy" who had failed to support a fellow sister and instead reduced her to tears. They were annoyed that our get-together had not been totally pleasurable, unemotional, dispassionate. I certainly felt miserable in the situation. The student, however, contacted me weeks later to share her feelings that she had gained new insights and awareness as a result of our encounter, which aided her personal growth. Incidents like this one, which initially appear to be solely negative because of tension or hostility, can lead to positive growth. If women always seek to avoid confrontation, to always be "safe," we may never experience any revolutionary change, any transformation, individually or collectively.

When women actively struggle in a truly supportive way to understand our differences, to change misguided, distorted perspectives, we lay the foundation for the experience of political solidarity. Solidarity is not the same as support. To experience solidarity, we must have a community of interests, shared beliefs, and goals around which to unite, to build Sisterhood. Support can be occasional. It can be given and just as easily withdrawn. Solidarity requires sustained, ongoing commitment. In feminist movement, there is need for diversity, disagreement, and difference if we are to grow. As Grace Lee Boggs and James Boggs emphasize in *Revolution and Evolution in the Twentieth Century*:

> The same appreciation of the reality of contradiction underlies the concept of criticism and self-criticism. Criticism and self-criticism are the way in which individuals united by common goals can consciously utilize their differences and limitations, i.e., the negative, in order to accelerate their positive advance. The popular formulation for this process is "changing a bad thing into a good thing."

Women do not need to eradicate difference to feel solidarity. We do not need to share common oppression to fight equally to end oppression. We do not need anti-male sentiments to bond us together, so great is the wealth of experience, culture, and ideas we have to share with one another. We can be sisters united by shared interests and beliefs, united in our appreciation for diversity, united in our struggle to end sexist oppression, united in political solidarity.

5

MEN
Comrades in Struggle

Feminism defined as a movement to end sexist oppression enables women and men, girls and boys, to participate equally in revolutionary struggle. So far, contemporary feminist movement has been primarily generated by the efforts of women—men have rarely participated. This lack of participation is not solely a consequence of anti-feminism. By making women's liberation synonymous with women gaining social equality with men, liberal feminists effectively created a situation in which they, not men, designated feminist movement "women's work." Even as they were attacking sex-role divisions of labor, the institutionalized sexism which assigns unpaid, devalued, "dirty" work to women, they were assigning to women yet another sex-role task: making feminist revolution. Women's liberationists called upon all women to join feminist movement, but they did not continually stress that men should assume responsibility for actively struggling to end sexist oppression. Men, they argued, were all-powerful, misogynist, oppressor—the enemy. Women were the oppressed—the victims. Such rhetoric reinforced sexist ideology by positing in an inverted form the notion of a basic conflict between the sexes, the implication being that the empowerment of women would necessarily be at the expense of men.

As with other issues, the insistence on a "woman only" feminist movement and a virulent anti-male stance reflected the race and class background of participants. Bourgeois white women, especially radical feminists, were envious of and angry at privileged white men for denying them an equal share in class privilege. In part, feminism provided them with a public forum for the expression of their anger as well as a political platform they could use to call attention to issues of social equality, demand change, and promote specific reforms. They were not eager to call attention to the fact that men do not share a common social status, that patriarchy does not negate the existence of class and race privilege or exploitation, that all men do not benefit equally from sexism. They did not want to acknowledge that bourgeois white women, though often victimized by sexism, have more power and privilege, are less likely to be exploited or oppressed, than poor, uneducated, non-white males. At the time, many white women's liberationists did not care about the fate of oppressed groups of men. In keeping with the exercise of race and/or class privilege, they deemed the life experiences of these men unworthy of their attention, dismissed them, and simultaneously deflected attention away from their support of continued exploitation and oppression. Assertions like "all men are the enemy" and "all men hate women" lumped all groups of men in one category, thereby suggesting that they share equally in all forms of male privilege. One of the first written statements that endeavored to make an anti-male stance a central feminist position was the "Redstockings Manifesto." Clause III of the manifesto reads:

> We identify the agents of our oppression as men. Male supremacy is the oldest, most basic form of domination. All other forms of exploitation and oppression (racism, capitalism, imperialism, etc.) are extensions of male supremacy: men dominate women, a few men dominate the rest. All power situations throughout history have been male-dominated and male-oriented. Men have controlled all political, economic, and cultural institutions and backed up this control with physical force. They have used their power to keep women in an inferior position. All men receive economic, sexual, and psychological benefits from male supremacy. All men have oppressed women.

Anti-male sentiments have alienated many poor and working-class women, particularly non-white women, from feminist movement.

Their life experiences have shown them that they have more in common with men of their race and/or class group than with bourgeois white women. They know the sufferings and hardships women face in their communities; they also know the sufferings and hardships men face, and they have compassion for them. They have had the experience of struggling with them for a better life. This has been especially true for black women. Throughout our history in the United States, black women have shared equal responsibility in all struggles to resist racist oppression. Despite sexism, black women have continually contributed equally to anti-racist struggle, and frequently, before contemporary black liberation effort, black men recognized this contribution. There is a special tie binding people together who struggle collectively for liberation. Black women and men have been united by such ties. They have known the experience of political solidarity. It is the experience of shared resistance struggle that led black women to reject the anti-male stance of some feminist activists. This does not mean that black women were not willing to acknowledge the reality of black male sexism. It does mean that many of us do not believe we will combat sexism or woman-hating by attacking black men or responding to them in kind.

Bourgeois white women cannot conceptualize the bonds that develop between women and men in liberation struggle and have not had as many positive experiences working with men politically. Patriarchal white male rule has usually devalued female political input. Despite the prevalence of sexism in black communities, the role black women play in social institutions, whether primary or secondary, is recognized by everyone as significant and valuable. In an interview with Claudia Tate, black woman writer Maya Angelou explains her sense of the different role black and white women play in their communities:

> Black women and white women are in strange positions in our separate communities. In the social gatherings of black people, black women have always been predominant. That is to say, in the church it's always Sister Hudson, Sister Thomas, and Sister Wetheringay who keep the church alive. In lay gatherings it's always Lottie who cooks, and Mary who's going to Bonita's where

there is a good party going on. Also, black women are the nurturers of children in our community. White women are in a different position in their social institutions. White men, who are in effect their fathers, husbands, brothers, their sons, nephews, and uncles, say to white women or imply in any case: "I don't really need you to run my institutions. I need you in certain places and in those places you must be kept—in the bedroom, in the kitchen, in the nursery, and on the pedestal." Black women have never been told this.

Without the material input of black women as participants and leaders, many male-dominated institutions in black communities would cease to exist; this is not the case in all white communities.

Many black women refused participation in feminist movement because they felt an anti-male stance was not a sound basis for action. They were convinced that virulent expressions of these sentiments intensify sexism by adding to the antagonism which already exists between women and men. For years black women (and some black men) had been struggling to overcome the tensions and antagonisms between black females and males that is generated by internalized racism (i.e., when the white patriarchy suggests one group has caused the oppression of the other). Black women were saying to black men, "We are not one another's enemy," "We must resist the socialization that teaches us to hate ourselves and one another." This affirmation of bonding between black women and men was part of anti-racist struggle. It could have been a part of feminist struggle had white women's liberationists stressed the need for women and men to resist the sexist socialization that teaches us to hate and fear one another. They chose instead to emphasize hate, especially male woman-hating, suggesting that it could not be changed. Therefore no viable political solidarity could exist between women and men. Women of color from various ethnic backgrounds, as well as women who were active in the gay movement, not only experienced the development of solidarity between women and men in resistance struggle, but recognized its value. They were not willing to devalue this bonding by allying themselves with anti-male, bourgeois white women. Encouraging political bonding between women and men to radically resist sexist oppression would have called attention to the transformative potential of feminism. The anti-male stance was a reactionary perspective that made feminism appear to be a movement that would enable white women to usurp white male power, replacing white male supremacist rule with white female supremacist rule.

Within feminist organizations, the issue of female separatism was initially separated from the anti-male stance; it was only as the movement progressed that the two perspectives merged. Many all-female, sex-segregated groups were formed because women recognized that separatist organizing could hasten female consciousness-raising, lay the groundwork for the development of solidarity among women, and generally advance the movement. It was believed that mixed groups would get bogged down by male power trips. Separatist groups were seen as a necessary strategy, not as a way to attack men. Ultimately, the purpose of such groups was integration with equality.

The positive implications of separatist organizing were diminished when radical feminists, like Ti-Grace Atkinson, proposed sexual separatism as an ultimate goal of feminist movement. Reactionary separatism is rooted in the conviction that male supremacy is an absolute aspect of our culture, that women have only two alternatives: accepting it or withdrawing from it to create subcultures. This position eliminates any need for revolutionary struggle, and it is in no way a threat to the status quo. In the essay "Separate to Integrate," Barbara Leon stresses that male supremacists would rather feminist movement remain "separate and unequal." She gives the example of orchestra conductor Antonia Brico's efforts to shift from an all-women orchestra to a mixed orchestra, only to find she could not get support for the latter:

> Antonia Brico's efforts were acceptable as long as she confined herself to proving that women were qualified musicians. She had no trouble finding 100 women who could play in an orchestra or getting financial backing for them to do so. But finding the backing for men and women to play together in a truly integrated orchestra proved to be impossible. Fighting for integration proved

to be more of a threat to male supremacy and, therefore, harder to achieve.

The women's movement is at the same point now. We can take the easier way of accepting segregation, but that would mean losing the very goals for which the movement was formed. Reactionary separatism has been a way of halting the push of feminism.

During the course of contemporary feminist movement, reactionary separatism has led many women to abandon feminist struggle, yet it remains an accepted pattern for feminist organizing, e.g., autonomous women's groups within the peace movement. As a policy, it has helped to marginalize feminist struggle, to make it seem more a personal solution to individual problems, especially problems with men, than a political movement that aims to transform society as a whole. To return to an emphasis on feminism as revolutionary struggle, women can no longer allow feminism to be another arena for the continued expression of antagonism between the sexes. The time has come for women active in feminist movement to develop new strategies for including men in the struggle against sexism.

All men support and perpetuate sexism and sexist oppression in one form or another. It is crucial that feminist activists not get bogged down in intensifying our awareness of this fact to the extent that we do not stress the more unemphasized point, which is that men can lead life-affirming, meaningful lives without exploiting and oppressing women. Like women, men have been socialized to passively accept sexist ideology. While they need not blame themselves for accepting sexism, they must assume responsibility for eliminating it. It angers women activists who push separatism as a goal of feminist movement to hear emphasis placed on men being victimized by sexism; they cling to the "all men are the enemy" version of reality. Men are not exploited or oppressed by sexism, but there are ways in which they suffer as a result of it. This suffering should not be ignored. While it in no way diminishes the seriousness of male abuse and oppression of women, or negates male responsibility for exploitative actions, the pain men experience can serve as a catalyst calling attention to the need for change. Recognition of the painful consequences of sexism in their lives led some men to establish consciousness-raising groups to examine this. Paul Hornacek explains the purpose of these gatherings in his essay "Anti-Sexist Consciousness-Raising Groups for Men":

> Men have reported a variety of different reasons for deciding to seek a C-R group, all of which have an underlying link to the feminist movement. Most are experiencing emotional pain as a result of their male sex role and are dissatisfied with it. Some have had confrontations with radical feminists in public or private encounters and have been repeatedly criticized for being sexist. Some come as a result of their commitment to social change and their recognition that sexism and patriarchy are elements of an intolerable social system that needs to be altered.

Men in the consciousness-raising groups Hornacek describes acknowledge that they benefit from patriarchy and yet are also hurt by it. Men's groups, like women's support groups, run the risk of overemphasizing personal change at the expense of political analysis and struggle.

Separatist ideology encourages women to ignore the negative impact of sexism on male personhood. It stresses polarization between the sexes. According to Joy Justice, separatists believe that there are "two basic perspectives" on the issue of naming the victims of sexism: "There is the perspective that men oppress women. And there is the perspective that people are people, and we are all hurt by rigid sex roles." Many separatists feel that the latter perspective is a sign of co-optation, representing women's refusal to confront the fact that men are the enemy—they insist on the primacy of the first perspective. Both perspectives accurately describe our predicament. Men do oppress women. People are hurt by rigid sex-role patterns. These two realities co-exist. Male oppression of women cannot be excused by the recognition that there are ways men are hurt by rigid sex roles. Feminist activists should acknowledge that hurt—it exists. It does not erase or lessen male responsibility for supporting and perpetuating their power under patriarchy to exploit and oppress women in a manner far more grievous than the psychological stress or emotional pain caused by male conformity to rigid sex-role patterns.

Women active in feminist movement have not wanted to focus in any way on male pain so as not to deflect attention away from the focus on male privilege. Separatist feminist rhetoric suggested that all men share equally in male privilege, that all men reap positive benefits from sexism. Yet the poor or working-class man who has been socialized via sexist ideology to believe that there are privileges and powers he should possess solely because he is male often finds that few, if any, of these benefits are automatically bestowed on him in life. More than any other male group in the United States, he is constantly concerned about the contradiction between the notion of masculinity he was taught and his inability to live up to that notion. He is usually "hurt," emotionally scarred because he does not have the privilege or power society has taught him "real men" should possess. Alienated, frustrated, pissed off, he may attack, abuse, and oppress an individual woman or women, but he is not reaping positive benefits from his support and perpetuation of sexist ideology. When he beats or rapes women, he is not exercising privilege or reaping positive rewards; he may feel satisfied in exercising the only form of domination allowed him. The ruling-class male power structure that promotes his sexist abuse of women reaps the real material benefits and privileges from his actions. As long as he is attacking women and not sexism or capitalism, he helps to maintain a system that allows him few, if any, benefits or privileges. He is an oppressor. He is an enemy to women. He is also an enemy to himself. He is also oppressed. His abuse of women is not justifiable. Even though he has been socialized to act as he does, there are existing social movements that would enable him to struggle for self-recovery and liberation. By ignoring these movements, he chooses to remain both oppressor and oppressed. If feminist movement ignores his predicament, dismisses his hurt, or writes him off as just another male enemy, then we are passively condoning his actions.

The process by which men act as oppressors and are oppressed is particularly visible in black communities, where men are working-class and poor. In her essay "Notes for Yet Another Paper on Black Feminism, or, Will the Real Enemy Please Stand Up?"

black feminist activist Barbara Smith suggests that black women are unwilling to confront the problem of sexist oppression in black communities:

> By naming sexist oppression as a problem it would appear that we would have to identify as threatening a group we have heretofore assumed to be our allies—Black men. This seems to be one of the major stumbling blocks to beginning to analyze the sexual relationships/sexual politics of our lives. The phrase "men are not the enemy" dismisses feminism and the reality of patriarchy in one breath and also overlooks some major realities. If we cannot entertain the idea that some men are the enemy, especially white men and in a different sense Black men, too, then we will never be able to figure out all the reasons why, for example, we are beaten up every day, why we are sterilized against our wills, why we are being raped by our neighbors, why we are pregnant at age twelve, and why we are at home on welfare with more children than we can support or care for. Acknowledging the sexism of Black men does not mean that we become "man-haters" or necessarily eliminate them from our lives. What it does mean is that we must struggle for a different basis of interaction with them.

Women in black communities have been reluctant to publicly discuss sexist oppression, but they have always known it exists. We too have been socialized to accept sexist ideology, and many black women feel that black male abuse of women is a reflection of frustrated masculinity—such thoughts lead them to see that abuse is understandable, even justified. The vast majority of black women think that just publicly stating that these men are the enemy or identifying them as oppressors would do little to change the situation; they fear it could simply lead to greater victimization. Naming oppressive realities, in and of itself, has not brought about the kinds of changes for oppressed groups that it can for more privileged groups, who command a different quality of attention. The public naming of sexism has generally not resulted in the institutionalized violence that characterized, for example, the response to black civil rights struggles. (Private naming, however, is often met with violent oppression.) Black women have not joined feminist movement not because they cannot face the reality of sexist oppression; they face it daily. They do not join feminist movement because they do not see in feminist theory and practice, especially those writings made available to masses of people, potential solutions.

So far, feminist rhetoric identifying men as the enemy has had few positive implications. Had feminist activists called attention to the relationship between ruling-class men and the vast majority of men, who are socialized to perpetuate and maintain sexism and sexist oppression even as they reap no life-affirming benefits, these men might have been motivated to examine the impact of sexism in their lives. Often feminist activists talk about male abuse of women as if it is an exercise of privilege rather than an expression of moral bankruptcy, insanity, and dehumanization. For example, in Barbara Smith's essay, she identifies white males as "the primary oppressor group in American society" and discusses the nature of their domination of others. At the end of the passage in which this statement is made she comments: "It is not just rich and powerful capitalists who inhibit and destroy life. Rapists, murderers, lynchers, and ordinary bigots do, too, and exercise very real and violent power because of this white male privilege." Implicit in this statement is the assumption that the act of committing violent crimes against women is either a gesture or an affirmation of privilege. Sexist ideology brainwashes men to believe that their violent abuse of women is beneficial when it is not. Yet feminist activists affirm this logic when we should be constantly naming these acts as expressions of perverted power relations, general lack of control over one's actions, emotional powerlessness, extreme irrationality, and, in many cases, outright insanity. Passive male absorption of sexist ideology enables them to interpret this disturbed behavior positively. As long as men are brainwashed to equate violent abuse of women with privilege, they will have no understanding of the damage done to themselves or the damage they do to others, and no motivation to change.

Individuals committed to feminist revolution must address ways that men can unlearn sexism. Women were never encouraged in contemporary feminist movement to point out to men their responsibility. Some feminist rhetoric "put down" women who related to men at all. Most women's liberationists were saying, "Women have nurtured, helped, and supported others for too long—now we must fend for ourselves." Having helped and supported men for centuries by acting in complicity with sexism, women were suddenly encouraged to withdraw their support when it came to the issue of "liberation." The insistence on a concentrated focus on individualism, on the primacy of self, deemed "liberatory" by women's liberationists, was not a visionary, radical concept of freedom. It did provide individual solutions for women, however. It was the same idea of independence perpetuated by the imperialist patriarchal state which equates independence with narcissism, and lack of concern with triumph over others. In this way, women active in feminist movement were simply inverting the dominant ideology of the culture—they were not attacking it. They were not presenting practical alternatives to the status quo. In fact, even the statement "men are the enemy" was basically an inversion of the male supremacist doctrine that "women are the enemy"—the old Adam and Eve version of reality.

In retrospect, it is evident that the emphasis on "man as enemy" deflected attention away from focus on improving relationships between women and men, ways for men and women to work together to unlearn sexism. Bourgeois women active in feminist movement exploited the notion of a natural polarization between the sexes to draw attention to equal-rights effort. They had an enormous investment in depicting the male as enemy and the female as victim. They were the group of women who could dismiss their ties with men once they had an equal share in class privilege. They were ultimately more concerned with obtaining an equal share in class privilege than with the struggle to eliminate sexism and sexist oppression. Their insistence on separating from men heightened the sense that they, as women without men, needed equality of opportunity. Most women do not have the freedom to separate from men because of economic interdependence. The separatist notion that women could resist sexism by withdrawing from contact with men reflected a bourgeois class perspective. In Cathy McCandless's essay "Some Thoughts about Racism, Classism, and Separatism," she makes the point that separatism is in many ways a false issue because "in this capitalist economy, none of us are truly separate." However, she adds:

> Socially, it's another matter entirely. The richer you are, the less
> you generally have to acknowledge those you depend upon.
> Money can buy you a great deal of distance. Given enough of it, it
> is even possible never to lay eyes upon a man. It's a wonderful
> luxury, having control over who you lay eyes on, but let's face it:
> most women's daily survival still involves face-to-face contact
> with men whether they like it or not. It seems to me that for this
> reason alone, criticizing women who associate with men not only
> tends to be counterproductive; it borders on blaming the victim.
> Particularly if the women taking it upon themselves to set the
> standards are white and upper- or middle-class (as has often been
> the case in my experience) and those to whom they apply these
> rules are not.

Devaluing the real necessities of life that compel many women to remain in contact with men, as well as not respecting the desire of women to keep contact with men, created an unnecessary conflict of interest for those women who might have been very interested in feminism but felt they could not live up to the politically correct standards.

Feminist writings did not say enough about ways women could directly engage in feminist struggle in subtle, day-to-day contacts with men, although they have addressed crises. Feminism is politically relevant to the masses of women who daily interact with men both publicly and privately if it addresses ways that interaction, which usually has negative components because sexism is so all-pervasive, can be changed. Women who have daily contact with men need useful strategies that will enable them to integrate feminist movement into their daily life. By inadequately addressing or failing to address the difficult issues, contemporary feminist movement located itself on the periphery of society rather than at the center. Many women and men think feminism is happening, or happened, "out there." Television tells them the "liberated" woman is an exception, that she is primarily a careerist. Commercials like the one that shows a white career woman shifting from work attire to flimsy clothing exposing flesh, singing all the while, "I can bring home the bacon, fry it up in the pan, and never let you forget you're a man," re-affirm that her careerism will not prevent her from assuming the stereotyped sex-object role assigned women in male supremacist society.

Often men who claim to support women's liberation do so because they believe they will benefit by no longer having to assume specific, rigid sex roles they find negative or restrictive. The role they are most willing and eager to change is that of economic provider. Commercials like the one described above assure men that women can be breadwinners or even "the" breadwinner, but still allow men to dominate them. Carol Hanisch's essay "Men's Liberation" explores the attempt by these men to exploit women's issues to their own advantage, particularly those issues related to work:

> Another major issue is the attempt by men to drop out of the work force and put their women to work supporting them. Men don't like their jobs, don't like the rat race, and don't like having a boss. That's what all the whining about being a "success symbol" or "success object" is really all about. Well, women don't like those things either, especially since they get paid 40% less than men for working, generally have more boring jobs, and rarely are even allowed to be "successful." But for women working is usually the only way to achieve some equality and power in the family, in their relationship with men, some independence. A man can quit work and pretty much still remain the master of the household, gaining for himself a lot of free time since the work he does doesn't come close to what his wife or lover does. In most cases, she's still doing more than her share of the housework in addition to wife work and her job. Instead of fighting to make his job better, to end the rat race, and to get rid of bosses, he sends his woman to work—not much different from the old practice of buying a substitute for the draft, or even pimping. And all in the name of breaking down "role stereotypes" or some such nonsense.

Such a "men's liberation movement" could only be formed in reaction to women's liberation in an attempt to make feminist movement serve the opportunistic interests of individual men. These men identified themselves as victims of sexism working to liberate men. They identified rigid sex roles as the primary source of their victimization, and, though they wanted to change the notion of masculinity, they were not particularly concerned with their sexist exploitation and oppression of women. Narcissism and general self-pity characterized men's liberation groups. Hanisch concludes her essay with the statement:

> Women don't want to pretend to be weak and passive. And we don't want phony, weak, passive-acting men any more than we want phony supermen full of bravado and little else. What women want is for men to be honest. Women want men to be bold—boldly honest, aggressive in their human pursuits. Boldly passionate, sexual, and sensual. And women want this for themselves. It's time men became boldly radical. Daring to go to the root of their own exploitation and seeing that it is not women or "sex roles" or "society" causing their unhappiness, but capitalists and capitalism. It's time men dare to name and fight these, their real exploiters.

Men who have dared to be honest about sexism and sexist oppression, who have chosen to assume responsibility for opposing and resisting it, often find themselves isolated. Their politics are disdained by anti-feminist men and women, and are often ignored by women active in feminist movement. Writing about his efforts to publicly support feminism in a local newspaper in Santa Cruz, Morris Conerly explains:

> Talking with a group of men, the subject of Women's Liberation inevitably comes up. A few laughs, snickers, angry mutterings, and denunciations follow. There is a group consensus that men are in an embattled position and must close ranks against the assaults of misguided females. Without fail, someone will solicit me for my view, which is that I am 100% for Women's Liberation. That throws them for a loop and they start staring at me as if my eyebrows were crawling with lice.
>
> They're thinking, "What kind of man is he?" I am a black man who understands that women are not my enemy. If I were a white man with a position of power, one could understand the reason for defending the status quo. Even then, the defense of a morally bankrupt doctrine that exploits and oppresses others would be inexcusable.

Conerly stresses that it was not easy for him to publicly support feminist movement, that it took time:

> Why did it take me some time? Because I was scared of the negative reaction I knew would come my way by supporting Women's Liberation. In my mind I could hear it from the brothers and sisters. "What kind of man are you?" "Who's wearing the pants?" "Why are you in that white shit?" And on and on. Sure enough the attacks came as I had foreseen but by that time my belief was firm enough to withstand public scorn.
>
> With growth there is pain...and that truism certainly applied in my case.

Men who actively struggle against sexism have a place in feminist movement. They are our comrades. Feminists have recognized and supported the work of men who take responsibility for sexist oppression—men's work with batterers, for example. Those women's liberationists who see no value in this participation must rethink and re-examine the process by which revolutionary struggle is advanced. Individual men tend to become involved in feminist movement because of the pain generated in relationships with women. Usually a woman friend or companion has called attention to their support of male supremacy. Jon Snodgrass introduces the book he edited, *For Men Against Sexism: A Book of Readings,* by telling readers:

> While there were aspects of women's liberation which appealed to men, on the whole my reaction was typical of men. I was threatened by the movement and responded with anger and ridicule. I believed that men and women were oppressed by capitalism, but not that women were oppressed by men. I argued that "men are oppressed too" and that it's workers who need liberation! I was unable to recognize a hierarchy of inequality between men and women (in the working class) nor to attribute it to male domination. My blindness to patriarchy, I now think, was a function of my male privilege. As a member of the male gender case, I either ignored or suppressed women's liberation.
>
> My full introduction to the women's movement came through a personal relationship.... As our relationship developed, I began to receive repeated criticism for being sexist. At

first I responded, as part of the male backlash, with anger and denial. In time, however, I began to recognize the validity of the accusation, and eventually even to acknowledge the sexism in my denial of the accusations.

Snodgrass participated in the men's consciousness-raising groups and edited the book of readings in 1977. Towards the end of the 1970s, interest in male anti-sexist groups declined. Even though more men than ever before support the idea of social equality for women, like women they do not see this support as synonymous with efforts to end sexist oppression, with feminist movement that would radically transform society. Men who advocate feminism as a movement to end sexist oppression must become more vocal and public in their opposition to sexism and sexist oppression. Until men share equal responsibility for struggling to end sexism, feminist movement will reflect the very sexist contradictions we wish to eradicate.

Separatist ideology encourages us to believe that women alone can make feminist revolution—we cannot. Since men are the primary agents maintaining and supporting sexism and sexist oppression, they can only be successfully eradicated if men are compelled to assume responsibility for transforming their consciousness and the consciousness of society as a whole. After hundreds of years of anti-racist struggle, more than ever before non-white people are currently calling attention to the primary role white people must play in anti-racist struggle. The same is true of the struggle to eradicate sexism—men have a primary role to play. This does not mean that they are better equipped to lead feminist movement; it does mean that they should share equally in resistance struggle. In particular, men have a tremendous contribution to make to feminist struggle in the area of exposing, confronting, opposing, and transforming the sexism of their male peers. When men show a willingness to assume equal responsibility in feminist struggle, performing whatever tasks are necessary, women should affirm their revolutionary work by acknowledging them as comrades in struggle.

6

CHANGING
PERSPECTIVES ON POWER

In this society, power is commonly equated with domination and control over people or things. Women active in feminist movement had ambivalent responses to the issue of power. On the one hand, they stressed women's powerlessness, condemning male exercise of power as domination, and on the other hand, they raised the banner of "woman power," demanding equal rights—equal protection in political arenas, equal access to economic wealth. When black woman activist Cellestine Ware titled her book on the movement for women's liberation *Woman Power,* she was referring to a radically different concept of power—the exercise of power to end domination, which she maintained was a central tenet of radical feminist movement:

> Radical feminism, and this by no means includes all positions within the Women's Liberation Movement, postulates that the domination of one human being by another is the basic evil in society. Dominance in human relationships is the target of their opposition.

Radical feminists challenged the prevailing notion of power as domination and attempted to transform its meaning. Yet their attempts were not successful. As feminist movement progressed, critiques of the notion of power as domination and control were submerged as bourgeois activists began to focus on women over-coming their fear of power (the implication being that if they wanted social equality with men, they would need to participate equally in exercising domination and control over others). Differing perspectives on power within feminist movement reflected individual class biases and political perspectives. Women interested in reforms that would lead to social equality with men wanted to obtain greater power in the existing system. Women interested in revolutionary change were quick to label the exercise of power a negative trait, without distinguishing between power as domination and control over others and power that is creative and life-affirming.

Books like Phyllis Chesler and Emily Jane Goodman's *Women, Money, and Power* emphasize women's powerlessness and argue in favor of women working to obtain power within the existing social structure, while remaining ambivalent about whether women's exercise of power would be any less corrupt or destructive than men's. In the epilogue, Chesler and Goodman point to the different perspectives on power that have emerged in feminist movement, raising a number of interesting questions. They write:

> Women rising to relative or absolute power within the existing structure might just imitate men, and in the process become the oppressors of other people, including other women. As an example, Margaret Thatcher, now leader of England's conservative party, made the budgetary decision to terminate the distribution of free milk to school children.
>
> Or, is there some possibility that once in power, women would overcome the established economic and social system and would be more humanist?... Do women lust for power? Do they really resist the pressure of ambition? Do they not care about working for themselves for society? Do women possess greater morals, more substantial values than men, or are they just as conditioned to relate to short-range personal goals, or do they just lack information?
>
> Do women not want the control, in some way, of human beings by other human beings? Do women resist job promotion because of their understanding of the moral compromise? Do

women question the moral justification, if any, for such
control—power?

These questions were not answered by the authors, yet they raise
many of the critical issues that must be addressed if feminist activists
are to understand women's relationship to power. Had they been
answered, it would have been apparent that women cannot gain
much power on the terms set by the existing social structure without
undermining the struggle to end sexist oppression.

In a note about the authors of *Women, Money, and Power,* Emily
Jane Goodman states, "The basic dilemma is how women can gain
enough money and power to literally change the world, without being corrupted, co-opted, and incorporated on the way by the very
value systems we must change." This statement shows either a lack
of understanding of the process by which individuals gain money
and power (they do so by embracing, supporting, and perpetuating
the dominant ideology of the culture) or a naive refusal to confront
this reality. Bourgeois white women active in feminist movement
presented their struggle to obtain power in the terms set by the existing social structure as a necessary prerequisite for successful feminist struggle. Their suggestion that they should first obtain money
and power so as to work more effectively for liberation had little appeal for poor and/or non-white women. It had tremendous appeal
for ruling groups of white males who were not threatened by
women in feminist movement validating the status quo.

Many participants in feminist movement sincerely believed
that women were different from men and would exercise power
differently. They had been socialized to accept a sexist ideology that
stressed such difference, and feminist ideology reaffirmed the primacy
of these differences. In *Women, Money, and Power* the authors comment:

> Women's values, or the values attributed to women, are different
> from those which run America. This may be out of politics, igno-
> rance, fear, or conditioning. Whatever the values women have pur-
> sued—have been allowed to pursue—they are not the same as men's.

Statements like this one were commonly expressed sentiments in
feminist circles. They mystify the true nature of women's experi-

ence. Women, though assigned different roles to play in society based on sex, are not taught a different value system. It is woman's overall acceptance of the value system of the culture that leads her to passively absorb sexism and willingly assume a pre-determined sex role. Although women do not have the power ruling groups of men often exert, they do not conceptualize power differently.

Like most men, most women are taught from childhood on that dominating and controlling others is *the* basic expression of power. Even though women do not yet kill in wars, do not shape government policy equally with men, they, along with male ruling groups and most men, believe in the dominant ideology of the culture. Were they to rule, society would not be organized that differently from the way it is currently organized. They would organize it differently only if they had a different value system. The issues around which women and men feel differently, illustrated recently by "the gender gap," do not constitute a different set of values. Feminist rhetoric pushing the notion of man as enemy and woman as victim enabled women to avoid doing the work of creating new value systems. Participants in feminist movement acted in accord with sexist mystification of women's experience by simply accepting that women are different from men, think and act differently, conceptualize power differently, and therefore have an inherently different value system. It simply is not so. For example, much has been made of the idea that women are nurturers who affirm life whereas men are the killers, the warriors, who negate life. Yet women act in nurturing roles even as they socialize young children as parents or educators to believe "might makes right," even as they exercise abusive domination and control over children, even as they physically abuse children in increasing numbers. When contradictions like this one are pointed out, the stereotypical feminist response is that these women are carrying out the orders of men, that they are male-identified. Narrowly focused feminist ideology tends to equate male development and perpetuation of oppressive policy with maleness; the two things are not synonymous. By making them synonymous, women do not have to face the drive for power in women that leads them to strive to dominate and control others. The responsibility for female commitment to domination and control over others can be simply placed on men. If women active in feminist movement had a different value system from that of men, they would not endorse domination and control over others under any circumstances; they would not accept the belief that "might makes right."

If more feminist women had actively reconceptualized power, they would not have, consciously or unconsciously, shaped feminist movement using the class and race hierarchies that exist in the larger society. They would not have encouraged women to emulate men, the so-called "enemy." Yet when bourgeois white women active in feminist movement sought role models who possess strength, confidence, assertiveness, and decision-making ability, they chose ruling groups of white males. They could have chosen to pattern their behavior after that of working-class women who possess these same qualities. In her essay "Class Realities: Create a New Power Base," Karen Kollias encouraged bourgeois women to see working-class women as role models:

> Lower and working-class women have been forced to surface their strengths in order to survive, and often have had to assume responsibility for others, as well. While most women have some elements of strength within them, many simply haven't had to develop it, because of their comfort and economic security.
>
> One of the major issues of the Women's Movement has been to eliminate women's weakness and replace it with confidence, independence. This is partly because middle-class women who have some kind of protector (a successful husband or father) feel a lack of control over their own lives and have felt the need to organize around that. This is valid within its own class context.
>
> Middle-class models of strength have primarily been men, and strength is usually equated with power. Lower- and working-class women, especially non-white women, on the other hand, have seldom been able to depend on someone else for their decisions and maintenance. The process of taking active control over their lives, and of influencing those close to them, has given them a lifetime of experience with decision-making of the most basic nature—survival. This decision-making becomes part of what makes for a strong self-concept.... It follows, then, that women

with strong self-concepts should be models for women seeking that confidence.

Poor and working-class women did not become the role models for bourgeois white women because they were not seen by them as exercising forms of power valued in this society. In other words, their exercise of strength was not synonymous with economic power. Their power is in no way linked to domination or control over others, and this is the form of power that many bourgeois women are intrigued by and fascinated with. It is this form of power that has surfaced in feminist organizations, disrupting and corrupting feminist movement.

Despairing of the possibility that feminist revolution will occur, many women, once committed to working to eliminate sexist oppression, now focus their attention on gaining as much power and privilege as they can within the existing social structure. Feminist activists now know that women are likely to exercise power in the same manner as men when they assume the same positions in social and political arenas. Feminist activism called attention to the need for social equality of the sexes, yet ruling groups of men are willing to endorse equal rights only if it is clear that the women who enter spheres of power will work to uphold and maintain the status quo. Ronald Reagan's appointment of Sandra Day O'Connor to the Supreme Court is a case in point. O'Connor is not supportive of most reforms that would enable women to have greater control over their lives, yet she wholeheartedly endorses policy decisions that maintain the status quo. Her appointment shows women, especially white women, that individual women can gain power and prestige in the existing structure if they support that structure. Undoubtedly, the Equal Rights Amendment would pass if ruling male groups were convinced that women with radical political perspectives would be outvoted, outnumbered, and silenced by conservative women—women like O'Connor who will exercise power alongside men even as they continue to support white supremacy, capitalism, and patriarchy. These women validate the concept of power as domination and control, and exercise it, while assuring men that their "masculinity" is in no way diminished.

Ruling male groups have been able to co-opt feminist reforms and make them serve the interests of the white supremacist, capitalist patriarchy because feminist activists naively assumed women were opposed to the status quo, had a different value system from men, and would exercise power in the interests of feminist movement. This assumption led them to pay no significant attention to creating alternative value systems that would include new concepts of power. Even though some feminist activists rejected the idea that women should obtain power on the terms set by the dominant ideology of the culture, they tended to see all power as evil. This reactionary response offered women no new ways to think about power and reinforced the idea that domination and control are the ultimate expressions of power. At the same time, other feminists did attempt to redefine power positively with new organizational strategies: rotating tasks, consensus, emphasis on internal democracy.

Nancy Hartsock's essay "Political Change: Two Perspectives on Power" describes the frustration that surfaced in feminist movement as women attempted to reconceptualize power. In her essay, she emphasizes understandings of power that are creative and life-affirming, definitions that equate power with the ability to act, with strength and ability, or with action that brings a sense of accomplishment. She comments:

> Significantly, these understandings of power do not require the domination of others; energy and accomplishment are understood to be satisfying in themselves. This kind of power is much closer to what the women's movement has sought...
>
> One source of the difficulties in the women's movement about leadership, strength, and achievement has been our lack of clarity about the differences between the two concepts of power. A letter of resignation from the women's movement, used by two different women in different cities, expresses some of the problems. They complain of being "labeled a thrill-seeking opportunist, a ruthless mercenary, out to make her fame and fortune over the dead bodies of selfless sisters." The letter argues that leader-

ship qualities should not be confused with the desire to be a leader, and, similarly, that achievement or productivity should not be confused with the desire to be a leader (by implication, to dominate others). These statements indicate that women have not recognized that power understood as energy, strength, and effective interaction need not be the same as power that requires the domination of others in the movement.

This essay appeared in the feminist quarterly *Quest* in the summer of 1974. It was published at a time when women active in feminist movement were more inclined to collectively question and criticize concepts of power than they are today. Potentially, the feminist challenge to power in everyday relationships, which led to a questioning of all forms of power, was radical. While different concepts of power are more frequently discussed at this time, it is the exercise of power as domination and control that prevails, that is seen as the most significant form of power. This is true in feminist circles.

Struggles for power (the right to dominate and control others) perpetually undermine feminist movement and are likely to hasten its demise. The idea of woman power rooted in the exercise of power to end domination is most often discussed in a sentimental context wherein the image of woman as life-affirming nurturer is extolled. In most feminist contexts, the emphasis is on women obtaining power on the terms set by society. This misguided approach to liberation is criticized by Grace Lee Boggs and James Boggs in their book *Revolution and Evolution in the Twentieth Century:*

> The labor movement in the '30s, and all the movements of the '50s and '60s, the black movement, the youth movement, and the women's movement, began by struggling for their own interests, but derived their momentum from the fact that their interests coincided with those of society as a whole.... In the end, each has become an interest group, concerned only with itself. While each may talk about Black Power, Women Power, Worker's Power, in the final analysis each is only talking about separation of powers, or "a piece of the action." None is talking about real power, which involves the reconstruction of the entire society for the benefit of the great majority and for the advancement of humanity.

Before women can work to reconstruct society, we must reject the notion that obtaining power in the existing social structure will necessarily advance feminist struggle to end sexist oppression. It may allow numbers of women to gain greater material privilege, control over their destiny and the destiny of others, all of which are important goals. It will not end male domination as a system. The suggestion that women must obtain power before they can effectively resist sexism is rooted in the false assumption that women have no power. Women, even the most oppressed among us, do exercise some power. These powers can be used to advance feminist struggle. Forms of power held by exploited and oppressed groups are described in Elizabeth Janeway's important work *Powers of the Weak*. One of the most significant forms of power held by the weak is "the refusal to accept the definition of oneself that is put forward by the powerful." Janeway calls this the "ordered use of the power to disbelieve." She explains:

> It is true that one may not have a coherent self-definition to set against the status assigned by the established social mythology, and that is not necessary for dissent. By disbelieving, one will be led toward doubting prescribed codes of behavior, and as one begins to act in ways that can deviate from the norm in any degree, it becomes clear that in fact there is not just one right way to handle or understand events.

Women need to know that they can reject the powerful's definition of their reality—that they can do so even if they are poor, exploited, or trapped in oppressive circumstances. They need to know that the exercise of this basic personal power is an act of resistance and strength. Many poor and exploited women, especially non-white women, would have been unable to develop positive self-concepts if they had not exercised their power to reject the powerful's definition of their reality.

Much feminist thought reflects women's acceptance of the definition of femaleness put forth by the powerful. Even though women organizing and participating in feminist movement were in no way passive, unassertive, or unable to make decisions, they perpetuated the idea that these characteristics were typical female traits, a perspective that mirrored male supremacist interpretations of women's reality. They did not distinguish between the passive role many women assume in relation to male peers and/or male authority figures, and the assertive, even domineering, role they assume in relation to one another, to children, or to those individuals, female or male, who have lower social status, whom they see as inferiors. This is only one example of the way in which feminist activists did not break with the simplistic view of women's reality as it was defined by powerful men. If they had exercised the power to disbelieve, they would have insisted upon pointing out the complex nature of women's experience, deconstructing the notion that women are necessarily passive or unassertive.

Failure to exercise the power of disbelief made it difficult for women to reject prevailing notions of power and envision new perspectives. While feminist activists urged women to work to acquire economic and political power, they did not offer guidance and wise counsel about the exercise of that power. Women were not cautioned to maintain the political awareness that their newly gained power would advance feminist movement only if it was consciously used with that purpose in mind. They were reluctant and sometimes unwilling to admit that gaining power in the form of wealth was synonymous with supporting the exploitation and oppression of underclass women and men, that such power is rarely used by individuals to empower these groups. Vivian Gornick makes this point in her essay "The Price of Paying Your Own Way," distinguishing between women gaining economic self-sufficiency and the accumulation of wealth:

> There is no way—none—for anyone in this society to make a great deal of money without exploiting other people. If I had my way, capitalism and the consumer society would end tomorrow; it produces nothing but greed and injustice. I would like to see a world in which material tastes and needs are kept to a minimum.... The idea that money brings power and independence is an illusion. What money usually brings is the need for more money.

Some women's liberationists encouraged women to believe that their individual achievements of success, money, and power (especially in spheres historically dominated by men) advance feminist movement. These women need to know their success has little impact on the social status of women collectively and does not lessen the severity of sexist oppression or eliminate male domination. Their individualism is dangerously narcissistic when it leads them to equate personal success with radical political movement. Individual achievements advance feminist movement if they serve the interests of collective feminist struggle as well as satisfying individual aspirations.

As long as the United States is an imperialist, capitalist, patriarchal society, no large female majority can enter the existing ranks of the powerful. Feminist movement is not advanced if women who can never be among those who rule and exercise domination and control are encouraged to focus on these forms of power and see themselves as victims. The forms of power that these women should exercise are those that will enable them to resist exploitation and oppression and free them to work at transforming society so that political and economic structures will exist that benefit women and men equally. Feminist activists must emphasize the forms of power these women exercise and show ways they can be used for their benefit. One form of power women exercise in the economic sphere is that of consumption. Boycotts have been used often as a strategy, successful in educational if not economic terms. If women all around the United States turned off their television sets for an extended period of time and purchased no products other than very basic necessities to protest exploitation of women (e.g., increasing representation of violence against women on TV), these actions would have significant political and economic consequences. Since women are not thoroughly organized and are daily manipulated by ruling male groups who profit from sexism and female consumerism, we have never exercised this power. Most women do not understand the forms of power they could exercise. They need political education for critical consciousness to show them ways to exercise the limited powers they possess.

So far, feminist writers concerned with emphasizing women's

lack of economic power devalue their roles as consumers. Phyllis Chesler feels women are powerless as consumers:

> Buying things is presumably a woman's province. Women do buy the daily domestic necessities and luxuries, but they are "small" items in terms of price, importance, the value of decision-making, and its effect upon the economy in general. Most men control or at least share in buying the "large" domestic items at home and even "larger" items for industry and government. Consumer power is real—when the consumer is organized, knowledgeable, and powerful enough to require "large" items such as nuclear warheads. Consumer power is only a myth when consumers like housewives and mothers are unorganized, uninformed, and only require "small" items.

While women do not buy nuclear warheads, neither do most men. Contrary to Chesler's assumption that the purchase of small items is insignificant, profit from the sale of women's fashion alone makes it one of the major industries in this economy. Endless purchases of small items can lead to enormous economic profit and power. As consumers, women have power, and if organized could use that power to improve women's social status.

Feminist movement would have had, and will have, a greater appeal for masses of women if it addresses the powers women exercise even as it calls attention to sexist discrimination, exploitation, and oppression. Feminist ideology should not encourage (as sexism has done) women to believe they are powerless. It should clarify for women the powers they exercise daily and show them ways these powers can be used to resist sexist domination and exploitation. Sexism has never rendered women powerless. It has either suppressed their strength or exploited it. Recognition of that strength, that power, is a step women together can take towards liberation.

7

RETHINKING
THE NATURE OF WORK

Attitudes towards work in much feminist writing reflect bourgeois class biases. Middle-class women shaping feminist thought assumed that the most pressing problem for women was the need to get outside the home and work—to cease being "just" housewives. This was a central tenet of Betty Friedan's groundbreaking book, *The Feminine Mystique*. Work outside the home, feminist activists declared, was the key to liberation. Work, they argued, would allow women to break the bonds of economic dependency on men, which would in turn enable them to resist sexist domination. When these women talked about work they were equating it with high-paying careers; they were not referring to low-paying jobs or so-called "menial" labor. They were so blinded by their own experiences that they ignored the fact that a vast majority of women were (even at the time *The Feminine Mystique* was published) already working outside the home, working in jobs that neither liberated them from dependence on men nor made them economically self-sufficient. Benjamin Barber makes this point in his critique of the women's movement, *Liberating Feminism*:

> Work clearly means something very different to women in search of an escape from leisure than it has to most of the human race for most of history. For a few lucky men, for far fewer women, work has occasionally been a source of meaning and creativity.

But for most of the race it remains even now forced drudgery in front of ploughs, machines, words, or numbers—pushing products, pushing switches, pushing papers to eke out the wherewithal of material existence.

Critiques like Barber's did not lead feminist thinkers at that time to re-examine their perspectives on women and work. Even though the notion of work as liberation had little significance for exploited, underpaid, working women, it provided ideological motivation for college-educated white women to enter, or re-enter, the work force. It gave many non-college-educated white women who had been taught that a woman's place is in the home the support to tolerate low-paying jobs, primarily to boost household incomes and break into personal isolation. They could see themselves as exercising new freedom. In many cases, they were struggling to maintain middle-class lifestyles that could no longer be supported solely by the income of husbands. Caroline Bird explains the motivating forces behind their entry into the work force in *The Two-Paycheck Marriage:*

> Whether professional or "pink collar" work, wives didn't think of themselves in the context of economic history. They had no idea they were creating a revolution and had no intention of doing so. Most of them drifted into jobs "to help out" at home, to save for the down payment on a house, buy clothes for the children, or to meet the rising expenses of college. They eagerly sought part-time jobs, work that wouldn't "interfere" with their families. Instead of keeping women at home, children of the 1970s were the expense that drove women to earn, for wives with children at home were more apt to be earning than women in general.

Although many of these women never participated in feminist movement, they did think of themselves as challenging the old-fashioned ideas about women's place.

Early feminist perpetuation of the notion "work liberates women" alienated many poor and working-class women, especially non-white women, from feminist movement for a number of reasons. Campaigns like "wages for housework," whose organizers simultaneously challenged sexist definitions of work and the economic structures of capitalism, did not succeed in radicalizing the public's view of feminist definitions of work. Barber was correct when he made the point that these women often desire to quit working because the work they do is not liberating:

> Among many poorer Americans, liberation means the freedom of a mother finally to quit her job—to live the life of a capitalist stay-at-home, as it were. Of course work for her has meant scrubbing floors or scouring toilets or sewing endless buttons on discount smocks, and has more to do with self-preservation than self-realization. Even the most debasing sort of menial labor can, it is true, be perceived as an escape from the pointed dilemmas of leisure—providing it is not compulsory. To be able to work and to have to work are two very different matters.

As workers, poor and working-class women knew from their experiences that work was neither personally fulfilling nor liberatory—that it was for the most part exploitative and dehumanizing. They were suspicious of bourgeois women's assertion that women would be liberated via work, and they were also threatened. They were threatened because they knew that new jobs would not be created for those masses of white women seeking to enter the work force, and they feared that they and men of their classes would lose jobs. Benjamin Barber agreed with them:

> When large numbers of relatively well-educated women enter a rigid labor market in which large numbers of relatively unskilled workers are already unemployed, their employment will probably spell joblessness for many at the bottom. Non-white young men between sixteen and thirty, who already comprise a large proportion of the unemployed, will find it tougher than ever to get a job. At this point the need to set priorities based on some objective measure of real suffering, oppression, and injustice becomes paramount, and the real costs of feminist insistence on the term "oppression" become visible. Sexism exists with and not in the place of racism and economic exploitation. Liberationists cannot expect the poor to look appreciatively on what appears to be a middle-class campaign to wrest still more jobs away from them.

Black women and men were among the first groups to express fears that the influx of married white women into the job market would mean fewer hirings of qualified black people, given the extent to which white supremacy has worked to prevent and exclude non-white people from certain jobs. By grouping white women of all classes with non-white people in affirmative-action programs, a system was effectively institutionalized that allowed employers to continue discriminating against non-white peoples and maintain white supremacy by hiring white women. Employers could satisfy affirmative-action guidelines without hiring any non-white people. While I was working towards a Ph.D. degree in English, I was continually told by my white professors and peers that I would be the first to get a job, that my blackness would make it easier for me to get a job. This always puzzled me since the majority of affirmative-action positions filled during the course of my years of study went to white women. When a black person (or another non-white individual) was hired it was assumed that no other people of color would ever be considered for positions—this was not the case with white women. Unfortunately, the feminist activism that argued white women were a minority helped create a situation wherein jobs once designated primarily for qualified non-whites could be given to white women, and thus many people of color felt that the feminist movement was a threat to their liberation struggles. Had white feminist activists urged that two categories be set up in affirmative-action programs—one for women distinct from oppressed ethnic groups seeking job equity—it would not have appeared that white women's liberationists were eager to advance their cause at the expense of non-white women and men.

The emphasis on work as the key to women's liberation led many white feminist activists to suggest women who worked were "already liberated." They were in effect saying to the majority of working women, "Feminist movement is not for you." By formulating feminist ideology in such a way as to make it appear irrelevant to working women, bourgeois white women effectively excluded them from the movement. They were then able to shape feminist movement to serve their class interests without having to confront the impact, whether positive or negative, proposed feminist reforms would have on the masses of working-class women. Taking their cues from white women, many black women pointed to their having always worked outside the home as an indication that they were already liberated and not in need of feminist movement. They should have been challenging the idea that *any* work would liberate women and demanding that feminist movement address the concerns of working women.

If improving conditions in the workplace for women had been a central agenda for feminist movement in conjunction with efforts to obtain better-paying jobs for women and finding jobs for unemployed women of all classes, feminism would have been seen as a movement addressing the concerns of all women. Feminist focus on careerism, getting women employed in high-paying professions, not only alienated masses of women from feminist movement; it also allowed feminist activists to ignore the fact that increased entry of bourgeois women into the work force was not a sign that women as a group were gaining economic power. Had they looked at the economic situation of poor and working-class women, they would have seen the growing problem of unemployment and increased entry of women from all classes into the ranks of the poor.

Now that many middle-class white women divorce and find they enter the ranks of the poor and working-class, feminist activists have begun to talk about the "feminization of poverty" and are calling attention to the economic plight of women in the United States. Barbara Ehrenreich and Karin Stallard's essay "The Nouveau Poor" calls attention to the increased entry of middle-class white women into the ranks of the poor and emphasizes that poverty among women of all classes increased from 1967 to 1978, years many people thought were economically prosperous times for women:

> The grim economic news belies the image of the '70s as women's "decade of liberation." For some women, in some ways, it was. Women who were young, educated, and enterprising beat a path into once-closed careers like medicine, law, college teaching, and middle management. In the media, the old feminine ideal of the suburban housewife with 2.3 children and a station wagon was re-

placed by the upwardly mobile career woman with attaché case and skirted suit. Television "anchorwomen" became as familiar as yesterday's news, chairmen became chairpersons, so that at times it seemed as if the only thing holding back any woman was a subnormal supply of "assertiveness." But, underneath the upbeat images, women as a class—young, old, black, white—were steadily losing ground, with those who were doubly disadvantaged, black and Hispanic women, taking the heaviest losses.

Unfortunately, it is no accident that white women have only recently begun to focus on these losses. Classism and racism shape women's perspectives in such a way that bourgeois white women saw no need to call attention to these losses when they were not likely to be among those deprived. Concurrently, much recent attention to the issues of women and poverty (among feminists and coming from the right) implies that it is somehow more tragic, more worthy of note, more a situation in need of change because increasing numbers of white, middle-class women are likely someday to enter the ranks of the poor. This approach to the issue of women and poverty privileges the plight of one group of women. It encourages women to examine the impact of unemployment, divorce, etc. on bourgeois white women rather than compelling us to examine women's overall economic position. Had feminist activists been observing the entire picture all along, it would not have come as such a surprise that women as a group are losing rather than gaining ground economically, and the problems could have been addressed sooner.

Approached in the right way, attacking poverty could become one of the issues that could unite women from various ethnic groups and cultural backgrounds. Ehrenreich and Stallard assert:

> The feminization of poverty—or, to put it the other way, the impoverishment of women—may be the most crucial challenge facing feminism today.

Ending economic exploitation of women could become the feminist agenda that would address the concerns of masses of women, thereby breaking down the barriers separating those small groups of women who actively participate in feminist organizations from the

larger group of women in society who have not participated in organized feminist struggle. It could transform feminist movement
so that it would no longer serve the class interests of a specific
group. A collective attempt to address the problem of women's
economic exploitation would focus on a number of issues. Some of
these issues might be devising ways working conditions within the
present system can be improved, though this will not radically
change capitalist patriarchy. This latter point is crucial. It is a point
Ehrenreich and Stallard avoid making. While they write numerous
paragraphs outlining the problem, they write one paragraph suggesting a possible solution:

> We need a feminist economic program, and that is no small order.
> An economic program that speaks to the needs of women will
> have to address some of the most deep-seated injustices of a
> business-dominated economy and a male-dominated society.
> Naming it will take us beyond the familiar consensus defined by
> the demand for equal rights—to new issues, new programs, and
> maybe new perspectives. Whether there are debates ahead or col-
> lective breakthroughs, they are long overdue; the feminization of
> poverty demands a feminist vision of a just and democratic society.

Ehrenreich and Stallard suggest that women should work to envision new economic programs, but they avoid explicitly criticizing
capitalism in this essay. We must accept that it is a system that depends on the exploitation of underclass groups for its survival. We
must accept that within that system, masses of women are and will
be victims of class oppression.

Most women active in feminist movement do not have radical
political perspectives and are unwilling to face these realities, especially when they, as individuals, gain economic self-sufficiency
within the existing structure. They are reluctant, even unwilling, to
acknowledge that supporting capitalist patriarchy or even a
non-sexist capitalist system would not end the economic exploitation of underclass groups. These women fear the loss of their material privilege. As more middle-class white women lose status and
enter the ranks of the poor, they may find it necessary to criticize

capitalism. One of the women described by Ehrenreich and Stallard acknowledges that "hard times have a remarkable way of opening your eyes."

As more women face the bankruptcy of the present economic system, we must strive to envision new economic programs while working to alleviate women's current economic plight through meaningful reforms. Efforts to create new jobs by shortening the work week should be supported. Women should support the efforts of couples to share one high-paying position. Women should work to bring an end to the "family wage" men receive. Women should support welfare and demand welfare reform. On a very basic level, women need to learn to manage whatever money they receive more effectively. Women need help to break their addiction to compulsive consumerism. Groups of women on specific jobs need to organize collectively to demand better working conditions. Often poor working conditions make low-paying jobs women hold unhealthy, unnecessarily dehumanizing, stressful, and depressing. Women who work in service jobs who do not know how to address job-related problems need somewhere they can go for guidance and advice. The list of possible reforms and progressive programs is endless. Although some of these issues are already being addressed, they could all benefit from added support. When women see that their economic concerns are a central agenda for feminist movement, they will be more inclined to examine feminist ideology.

Women are exploited economically in jobs, but they are also exploited psychologically. They are taught via sexist ideology to devalue their contributions to the labor force. They are taught via consumerism to believe that they work solely out of material necessity or scarcity, not to contribute to society, to exercise creativity, or to experience the satisfaction of performing tasks that benefit oneself as well as others. Feminist focus on rethinking the nature of work would help women workers resist psychological exploitation even though such efforts would not change the economic situation. By attributing value to all the work women do, whether paid or unpaid, feminist activists would provide alternative self-concepts and self-definitions for women. All too often, focus on professions and careers within feminist movement led participants to act as if all other jobs, especially those that are low-paying, have no value. In this way, feminist attitudes towards work done by the masses of women mirrored the attitudes of men.

Many women in the job market do service work, which is either low-paying or unpaid (i.e., housework). Housework and other service work is particularly devalued in capitalist patriarchy. Feminist activists who argued for wages for housework saw this as a means of giving women some economic power and attributing value to the work they do. It seems unlikely that wages for housework would have led society to attribute value to these tasks since paid service work is seen as valueless. In paid service jobs, workers are compensated economically, but these compensations do not lessen the extent to which they are psychologically exploited. Their work has the same degrading stigma that is attached to housework. The anonymous authors of *Women and the New World* suggest that wages for housework is "a proposal that takes us even further down the road of capitalism since it brings us into the marketplace and puts a price on activities which should fulfill human needs and not just economic independence for women." Were women to receive wages for housework, it is unlikely that it would ever cease to be designated "woman's work," and it is unlikely that it would be regarded as valuable labor.

There have been too few works written about the value of service work and of housework in particular. (Ann Oakley's *The Sociology of Housework,* Rae André's *Homemakers: The Forgotten Workers,* and one anthology, *The Politics of Housework,* edited by Ellen Malos, are books about housework.) Yet there are few feminist studies that examine the extent to which well-done housework contributes to individual well-being, promotes the development of aesthetics, or aids in the reduction of stress. By learning housework, children and adults accept responsibility for ordering their material reality. They learn to appreciate and care for their surroundings. Since so many male children are not taught housework, they grow to maturity with no respect for their environment and often lack the know-how to take care of themselves and their households. They have been allowed to cultivate an unnecessary dependence on women in their domestic lives, and, as a result of this dependence, are sometimes unable to develop a healthy sense of autonomy. Girl children, though usually compelled to do housework, are usually taught to see it as demeaning and degrading. These attitudes lead them to hate doing housework and deprive them of the personal satisfaction that they could feel as they accomplish these necessary tasks. They grow to maturity with the attitude that most work, not just housework, is drudgery, and spend their time fantasizing about lives in which they do not do work, especially service work. Were they taught to value housework, they might approach all work differently. They might see work as an affirmation of one's identity rather than a negation. Today, many young Westerners, female and male, follow the teachings of varied Eastern religious and philosophical thought in the hopes of experiencing self-realization. During this process, they learn to re-think their attitudes towards work, especially service work. They learn that discipline begins with careful performance of all tasks, especially those deemed "menial" in this culture.

rethinking the nature of work is essential for feminist movement in the United States. As part of that rethinking, women must learn to value work. Many feminist activists did not take the position that it would be a significant and meaningful gesture of power and resistance for women to learn to value the work they do, whether paid or unpaid. They acted as if work done by women could only be deemed valuable if men, especially ruling groups of men, were compelled to acknowledge its value (in the case of housework, by making it wage labor). Whether men acknowledge the value of the work women do is irrelevant if women do not value that work.

Women, like other exploited and oppressed groups in this society, often have negative attitudes towards work in general and the work they do in particular. They tend to devalue the work they do because they have been taught to judge its significance solely in terms of exchange value. Receiving low wages or no wages is seen as synonymous with personal failure, lack of success, inferiority. Like other exploited groups, women internalize the powerful's definition of themselves and the powerful's estimation of the value of their labor. They do not develop an attitude towards work that sees it as an expression of dignity, discipline, creativity, etc. In *Revolution and Evolution in the Twentieth Century,* Grace Lee Boggs and James Boggs suggest that most workers in this society, female and male, think of work as a form of slavery and need to know that they create their humanity through participation in work:

> It is inconceivable that humankind could exist without work. The new ethic of work starts out in the first place with the idea that work is a necessity for the human personality. But man/woman has struggled for so long against compulsory work that we have lost the notion that if we didn't work, we would not exist as humans. We exist at the historical conjunction of the highest point of the mass struggle against labor and the technological revolution which eliminated the old reasons to work. So we have to re-affirm that people have to work, but they don't have to work in the old way and for the old reasons. We can't look for a new way or for new reasons unless we believe that there are human reasons for working...
>
> We need to set up a polarization, an opposition between two attitudes towards work. Whether or not one calls these respectively the "bourgeois" and the "socialist" attitudes to work is not important as long as we recognize that at this historical juncture, this transition, there are two attitudes: one which is hatred and repudiation of work, destructive of the human personality, and the other which recognizes work as essential to the development of oneself as a human being.

Traditionally, work has not been a sphere of human activity women have participated in for the purposes of developing their personalities, self-concepts, etc. This is one of the reasons why those who have achieved economic self-sufficiency are often as unable to liberate themselves from oppressive interactions with sexist individuals as those women who do no wage labor and depend on others for their economic survival. These working women often think that interpersonal relationships are the area in which they will develop personality, self-definition, etc. They may cling to the notion that they will someday be liberated from the need to work by meeting the "right" man. Such thinking leads them to support and perpetuate sexist ideology. Like working-class women, they could benefit from feminist effort to rethink the nature of work. Women who cannot find work, who are unemployed and compelled to rely on welfare, are encouraged by the ruling groups to see themselves as parasites living off the labor of others. The welfare system is structured to ensure that recipients will undergo a process of demoralization in order to receive aid. This process often creates depressions that paralyze these women and make them unable to liberate themselves from the position of dependents. These women could also benefit from feminist efforts to rethink the nature of work. They could participate in feminist-promoted efforts to restructure the current welfare system to link it to a positive concept of work, to ensure that it leads to jobs.

Future feminist movement will be sustained only if the needs of masses of women are addressed. By working to rethink the nature of work, feminist activists will be shaping the direction of the movement so that it will be relevant to all women and lead them to participate.

8

EDUCATING WOMEN
A Feminist Agenda

Many participants in contemporary feminist movement are college-educated. It is easy to assume our educational status and privilege are common among women and as a consequence we have not stressed the need to make education, especially basic literacy, a feminist agenda. Although feminist activists have focused on struggling against sexism in educational institutions and childhood socialization, they have not explored deeply the connection between sexist exploitation of women in this society and the degree of women's education, including the lack of basic reading and writing skills. Feminist activist and scholar Charlotte Bunch emphasizes the political importance of literacy in her essay "Feminism and Education":

> Revolutionary movements have almost always seen developing a general literacy as one of the most important tasks. Yet in this country, where we assume that most of us can read and write, it is often overlooked...
>
> Reading and writing are valuable in and of themselves, and women should have access to their pleasure. Beyond that, they are vital to change for several reasons. First, they provide a means of conveying ideas and information that may not be readily available in the popular media. For example, the idea of women's liberation first spread through mimeographed articles.... Second, reading and writing help develop an individual's imagination and ability to think.... Third, an individual's access, through reading a variety of interpretations of reality, increases that person's capac-

ity to think for herself, to go against the norms of the culture, and to conceive of alternatives for society—all of which are fundamental to acting politically. Fourth, reading and writing aid each woman's individual survival and success in the world, by increasing her ability to function in her chosen endeavors. And finally, the written word is still the cheapest and most accessible form of mass communication.... When we recall why literacy is important to movements, it becomes clear that we should neither assume that women are already literate, nor ignore the value of teaching women to read, write, and think as part of feminist education.

Class biases led women organizing feminist movement to simply assume that feminist theory and strategy would be best disseminated to masses of women via written materials. The focus on written material actually prohibits many women from learning about feminism. There are places in the United States where feminist literature is not available, where women and men have never heard the word "feminism" or have heard it and do not know what it really means. Had feminist activists engaged in charting the movement's direction considered the issue of literacy, they would have known that the emphasis on written material would make feminist ideas accessible to certain classes and groups of women. They would have known that a movement depending on the written word to carry its message would need to stress programs enabling all women to learn reading and writing. The political importance of literacy is still understressed in feminist movement today even though printed material has practically become the sole medium for expression of theory. Many theorists do not even intend their ideas to reach a mass public, and consequently we must take some responsibility for the superficial and perverted versions of feminist ideas that end up in the public imagination, via TV, for example. It is not too late for feminist activists to emphasize literacy and to organize literacy training programs for women. Through feminist-headed literacy programs, illiterate women from all classes, and especially those from poor and working-class backgrounds, could learn to read and write in conjunction with learning how to think critically and analytically.

Given the bourgeois class biases of many feminist activists, attention has been given to women in higher education, both as students and teachers, with little or no attention given to the need to
educate women who lack basic skills. Time and money have been
expended creating resources for women scholars and academics to
pursue and promote their work. While this effort is important, it
should not have greater priority than the struggle to ensure that all
women read and write. Given the many financial cutbacks taking
place on all levels in the United States, it is unlikely that women
could rely on public funding to establish literacy programs. However, programs could be sponsored by financial contributions from
women and men in academic institutions who are committed to radical political change. Even if funding were not available from any
source, small literacy programs could begin in neighborhoods and
communities where politically committed, skilled individuals could
teach women reading and writing.

Until masses of women in this society read and write, feminist
ideas must also be spread by word of mouth. Many women will not
leave or are unable to leave their homes to attend feminist conferences and public talks; door-to-door contact would serve as one way
feminist ideas could be shared. This contact could be made by
groups of women who are already participating in feminist organizations. Many women's studies students at universities all around the
United States grapple with the issue of whether or not their intellectual and scholarly pursuits are relevant to women as a collective
group, to women in the "real" world. Were these students to go into
communities and discuss feminist issues door-to-door, they would
be working to bridge the gap between their educational experiences
and the educational experiences of masses of women.

Many women are frightened by the thought of approaching
women who are strangers. One semester I taught a course in a
women's studies program called "Third World Women in the
United States," and though the ethnic background of the students
varied from semester to semester, this particular semester the students were almost all white. All the students lamented the absence
of larger numbers of women of color. I assigned them the project of

talking to non-white women on the campus about their reasons for not taking women's studies classes. They were encouraged to invite students to visit the classes. At first students were uncomfortable with the assignment. They were uneasy about approaching women they did not know. Most of them found that the women they spoke with often gave lack of information about courses and teachers as their primary reason for never taking a women's studies course. After the students reported their findings (some did bring groups of non-white women to class), we discussed ways all students could learn more about the women's studies program. While everyone agreed that printed publicity (ads in the school newspaper or posters) was a good strategy, we decided that talking with women about the courses was the most effective method. In dialogues, women could ask questions and thus dispel stereotypes or fears they might have about feminism and the women's studies program. The importance of verbal communication holds true for the dissemination of feminist ideas. In a door-to-door campaign to reintroduce feminist politics to a wider audience, women would have the opportunity to ask questions, clarify issues, give feedback. If, in a single year, women stopped spending thousands of dollars to organize conferences that are attended by only a select group of individuals, the goal of that year could be mass outreach in every state, with the intention of taking feminism out of the university and into the streets and homes of this society.

Feminist education has become institutionalized in universities via women's studies programs. While these programs are necessary and are an extremely effective way to teach college students about feminism, they have very little impact, if any, on masses of women and men. There are very few corresponding women's studies programs that make the same knowledge and information available to people who are not college students. Many students, female and male, find they do much of their rethinking of sexist socialization in women's studies classes. Usually the information they receive radically alters their perspectives on reality and changes their view of the nature of sex roles. This kind of information needs to reach more people. As part of her or his political commitment to feminism, a positive praxis for any academic would be offering women's studies courses at a local community center, YWCA, YMCA, church, etc. Even if they did not teach as many hours or days as they did at the university, any amount of time spent making women's studies available to the public would be significant.

During this past year I returned to the small Kentucky town I grew up in to give a talk, "Black Women Writers: The Vision of Community," during Black History Week. The talk was meant to highlight the way in which black women writers draw on elements of everyday life experiences in black homes and communities. Accustomed to teaching college courses where students are familiar with the literature, I found it challenging to devise a lecturing strategy that would make the same knowledge available to women and men (mainly African American) of all ages, literate and illiterate, many of whom were unfamiliar with the works and authors to be discussed. I relied heavily on reading passages from various texts—poetry, fiction, drama—using passages that involved unusual, exciting descriptions of everyday events. While I was preparing the talk, I was conscious of the desire not to "talk down" to the audience in any way. I wanted to keep the same intellectual level I would have in the college-classroom lecture. With this in mind, I began to think in terms of translation—giving the same message, using a different style, simpler sentence structures, etc.

The ability to "translate" ideas to an audience that varies in age, sex, ethnicity, and degree of literacy is a skill feminist educators need to develop. Concentration of feminist educators in universities encourages habitual use of an academic style that may make it impossible for teachers to communicate effectively with individuals who are not familiar with either academic style or jargon. All too often educators, especially university professors, fear their work will not be valued by other academics if it is presented in a way that makes it accessible to a wider audience. If these educators thought of rendering their work in a number of different styles, "translations," they would be able to satisfy arbitrary academic standards while making their work available to masses of people. Difficulty of access has been a problem with much feminist theory. A feminist essay with revolutionary ideas written in a complicated, abstract manner using the jargon of a specific discipline will not have the impact it should have on the consciousness of women and men because it will probably be read by only a small group of people. While feminist scholars should feel free to write using complex styles, if they are sincerely concerned with addressing their ideas to as many people as possible, they must either write in a more accessible manner or write in the manner of their choice and see to it that the piece is made available to others using a style that can be easily understood.

The value of a feminist work should not be determined by whether or not it conforms to academic standards. The value of a feminist work should not be determined by whether or not it is difficult reading. Concurrently, works should not be dismissed simply because they are difficult. If feminist writing and scholarship aim to promote and advance feminist movement, then matters of style must be considered in conjunction with political intent. There will be no mass-based feminist movement as long as feminist ideas are understood only by a well-educated few. The educational needs of the undereducated woman must be considered by feminist activists if the written word remains the primary medium for the dissemination of feminist ideas.

Another reason education has not been of primary concern to feminist activists is the tug-of-war that has existed within feminist movement between feminist intellectuals and academics, and participants in the movement who equate education with bourgeois privilege and are fiercely anti-intellectual. This tug-of-war has led to the formation of a false dichotomy between theory (the development of ideas) and practice (the actions of the movement), with one group privileging "practice." As a consequence, there is often little congruity between feminist theory and feminist practice. This intensifies the feelings of some women engaged in activism (like organizing a defense committee for a woman jailed for killing an abusive spouse) that they are superior to or more "politically correct" than women who concentrate their energies on developing ideas. From the onset, women's liberation movement participants have struggled to unite theory and practice, to create a liberatory feminist praxis (defined by Paulo Freire as "action and reflection upon the world in order to transform it"). That struggle has been undermined by anti-intellectualism and by elitist academics who believe their "ideas" need not have any connection to real life.

Bourgeois class biases have led many feminist theorists to develop ideas that have little or no relation to the lived experiences of most women, theories that are not useful for making feminist revolution. Annoyed and angered by these ideas, many women dismiss all theory as irrelevant. Yet women need to know that ideas and theories are important and absolutely essential for envisioning and making a successful feminist movement, one that will mobilize groups of people to transform this society. Ironically, lack of knowledge about revolutionary politics leads women to see ideas and theories as unimportant. In their chapter "Dialectics and Revolution," Grace Lee Boggs and James Boggs discuss the importance of ideas to revolutionary activists:

> Revolutionists seek to change reality, to make it better. Therefore, revolutionists not only need the revolutionary philosophy of dialectics. They need a revolutionary ideology, i.e. a body of ideas based on analyzing the main contradictions of the particular society which they are trying to change, projecting a vision of a higher form of reality in which this contradiction would be resolved, and relating this resolution to a social force or forces responsible for and capable of achieving it. It is only after you have arrived at the correct ideology that it makes sense to develop your revolutionary politics, i.e. the programs necessary to mobilizing and organizing the revolutionary social forces. If your ideology is wrong, i.e. misdirected or limited, then all the most brilliant programs for militant activity must be absolutely clear about this sequence—from revolutionary philosophy, to revolutionary ideology, to revolutionary politics.

Support of anti-intellectualism in feminist movement is a good example of ideology that undermines and impedes progress. As a group, women have been denied (via sex, race, and class exploitation and oppression) the right and privilege to develop intellectually. Most women are deprived of access to modes of thought that promote the kind of critical and analytical understanding necessary for liberation struggle. This deprivation leads women to feel insecure about intellectual work and to fear grappling with new ideas and information. It may lead us to dismiss as irrelevant that which is relevant because it is challenging.

Often women of color active in feminist movement are anti-intellectual. Many of us have not had access to university educations and do not hold advanced degrees. We may equate white female hegemonic dominance of feminist theory and practice with educational status. We may not attack that hegemony (which stems from class and race hierarchies) but instead "put down" intellectual work. By dismissing theory and privileging organization work, some women of color are able to see themselves as more politically engaged where it really counts. Yet by buying into this dichotomy between theory and practice, we place ourselves always on the side of the experiential, and in so doing support the notion (too often fostered by white women) that their role is to do the "brain" work, developing ideas, theories, etc., while our role is to do either the "dirty" work or to contribute the experience to validate and document their analysis. Women of color need to develop intellectually. While we need not be ashamed of not having certain educational skills, we need to assume responsibility for urging and helping one another combine organizational, practical skills with intellectual expertise. We need to examine why there are so few images of intellectual women who are non-white. Those of us who are educated, who hold advanced degrees, need to examine why we devalue intellectual activity. Women of color and all women from non-privileged backgrounds who are well-educated, who understand the value of intellectual development, the extent to which it strengthens any oppressed person who is seeking self-recovery and radical political change, must share their awareness with all women. We must actively struggle to rid feminist movement of its anti-intellectual bias. We must continue to criticize meaningless intellectual work and promote the kind of study and scholarship that is itself a feminist praxis.

In her writing, Charlotte Bunch encourages women to accept the challenge of education, whether it be the basic struggle for reading and writing skills or the struggle to develop critical and analytical skills. Writing about women's negative attitudes towards theory, Bunch comments:

> When teaching feminist theory, one must counter such attitudes and find ways to encourage women to think systematically about the world. Our society (and indeed all societies today) trains only a few people to think in this manner, mostly those from the classes it expects to control the social order. Certainly most women are not expected to take control, and, in consequence, are not encouraged to think analytically. In fact, critical thinking is the antithesis of woman's traditional role. Women are supposed to worry about mundane survival problems, to brood about fate, and to fantasize in a personal manner. We are not meant to think analytically about society, to question the way things are, or to consider how things could be different. Such thinking involves an active, not a passive, relationship to the world. It requires confidence that your thoughts are worth pursuing and that you can make a difference.... My goal in teaching feminist theory is to provoke women to think about their lives and society in this way.

Encouraging women to strive for education, to develop their intellects, should be a primary goal of feminist movement.

Education as "the practice of freedom" (to use another Freire phrase) will be a reality for women only when we develop an educational methodology that addresses the needs of all women. This is an important feminist agenda.

9

FEMINIST MOVEMENT
TO END VIOLENCE

Contemporary feminist movement successfully called attention to the need to end male violence against women. Shelters for abused and battered women were founded all around the United States by women activists dedicated to helping victimized women heal themselves and begin new lives. Despite years of committed hard work, the problem of male violence against women steadily increases. It is often assumed by feminist activists that this violence is distinct from other forms of violence in this society because it is specifically linked to the politics of sexism and male supremacy: the right of men to dominate women. In Susan Schechter's thorough study of the battered women's movement, *Women and Male Violence,* she continually emphasizes "that violence against women is rooted in male domination." Her chapter "Towards an Analysis of Violence Against Women in the Family" examines the extent to which the ideology of male supremacy both encourages and supports violence against women:

> Theoretical explanations for battering are not mere exercises; by pinpointing the conditions that create violence against women, they suggest the directions in which a movement should proceed to stop it. Woman abuse is viewed here as an historical expression of male domination manifested within the family and currently reinforced by the institutions, economic arrangements, and sexist

division of labor within capitalist society. Only by analyzing this total context of battering will women and men be able to devise a long-range plan to eliminate it.

While I agree with Schechter that male violence against women in the family is an expression of male domination, I believe that violence is inextricably linked to all acts of violence in this society that occur between the powerful and the powerless, the dominant and the dominated. While male supremacy encourages the use of abusive force to maintain male domination of women, it is the Western philosophical notion of hierarchical rule and coercive authority that is the root cause of violence against women, of adult violence against children, of all violence between those who dominate and those who are dominated. It is this belief system that is the foundation on which sexist ideology and other ideologies of group oppression are based; they can be eliminated only when this foundation is eliminated.

It is essential for continued feminist struggle to end violence against women that this struggle be viewed as a component of an overall movement to end violence. So far feminist movement has primarily focused on male violence, and as a consequence lends credibility to sexist stereotypes that suggest men are violent, women are not; men are abusers, women are victims. This type of thinking allows us to ignore the extent to which women (with men) in this society accept and perpetuate the idea that it is acceptable for a dominant party or group to maintain power over the dominated by using coercive force. It allows us to overlook or ignore the extent to which women exert coercive authority over others or act violently. The fact that women may not commit violent acts as often as men does not negate the reality of female violence. We must see both men and women in this society as groups who support the use of violence if we are to eliminate it.

The social hierarchy in white supremacist, capitalist patriarchy is one in which theoretically men are the powerful, women the powerless; adults the powerful, children the powerless; white people the powerful, black people and other non-white peoples the powerless. In a given situation, whichever party is in power is likely to use coercive authority to maintain that power if it is challenged or threatened. Although most women clearly do not use abuse and battery to control and dominate men (even though a small minority of women batter men), they may employ abusive measures to maintain authority in interactions with groups over whom they exercise power. Many of us who were raised in patriarchal homes where male parents maintained domination and control by abusing women and children know that the problem was often exacerbated by the fact that women also believed that a person in authority has the right to use force to maintain authority. Some of the women in these families exerted coercive authority over their children (as do women in families where men are not violent), sometimes with random acts of violent aggression for no clear reason or through systematic verbal abuse. This violence is not unlike male violence against children and women, even though it may not be as prevalent (which seems unlikely since 90 percent of all parents use some form of physical force against children). While it in no way diminishes the severity of the problem of male violence against women to emphasize that women are likely to use coercive authority when they are in power positions, recognizing this reminds us that women, like men, must work to unlearn socialization that teaches us it is acceptable to maintain power by coercion or force. By concentrating solely on ending male violence against women, feminist activists may overlook the severity of the problem. They may encourage women to resist male coercive domination without encouraging them to oppose all forms of coercive domination.

In a section of her theoretical chapter analyzing violence against women in the family, "Questions in Theory Building," Schechter acknowledges a need for further investigation of factors that cause battery. She points to the fact that women in lesbian relationships are sometimes battered to raise the question of how this information "fits" with a theory of battery that sees male domination as the cause. She answers, "One could theorize that models of intimate relationships based on power and domination are so pervasive in this society that they do, in fact, affect the nature of relationships between people of the same sex." Yet she is reluctant to accept this theory as it does not affirm male domination as the cause of battery. So she suggests that there must be greater research before the two forms of battery could be linked. However, if one assumes, as I do, that battery is caused by the belief permeating this culture that hierarchical rule and coercive authority are natural, then all our relationships tend to be based on power and domination, and thus all forms of battery are linked. In *The Cultural Basis of Racism and Group Oppression,* philosopher John Hodge suggests that it is in the context of the traditional Western family, with its authoritarian male rule and its authoritarian adult rule, that most of us are socialized to accept group oppression and the use of force to uphold authority. These patterns form the basis of all our relationships:

> Most personal relationships in Dualist culture take place within the established institutions. Consequently, most personal relationships contain a strong hierarchical element. Most personal interaction occurs within hierarchical structures and is shaped by these structures. We have just considered the relationship usually prevalent in the family where adult rule over non-adults and male rule over females is the accepted norm. In addition to these personal relationships, other personal interactions usually occur with the hierarchical framework of employer to employee, of boss or foreman to workers or crew, of producer or owner to user, of landlord to tenant, of lender to borrower, of teacher to student, of governor to governed—in short, of controller to controlled.

In all these relationships, the power the dominant party exercises is maintained by the threat (acted upon or not) that abusive punishment, physical or psychological, could be used if the hierarchical structure is threatened.

Male violence against women in personal relationships is one of the most blatant expressions of the use of abusive force to maintain domination and control. It epitomizes the actualization of the concept of hierarchical rule and coercive authority. Unlike violence against children, or white racial violence against other ethnic groups, it is the violence that is most overtly condoned and accepted, even celebrated in this culture. Society's acceptance and perpetuation of that violence helps maintain it and makes it difficult to control or eliminate. That acceptance can be explained only in part by patriarchal rule supporting male domination of women through the use of force. Patriarchal male rule took on an entirely different character in the context of advanced capitalist society. In the precapitalist world, patriarchy allowed all men to completely rule women in their families, to decide their fate, to shape their destiny. Men could freely batter women with no fear of punishment. They could decide whom their daughters were to marry, whether they would read or write, etc. Many of these powers were lost to men with the development of the capitalist nation-state in the United States. This loss of power did not correspond with decreased emphasis on the ideology of male supremacy. However, the idea of the patriarch as worker, providing for and protecting his family, was transformed as his labor primarily benefited the capitalist state.

Men not only no longer had complete authority and control over women; they no longer had control over their own lives. They were controlled by the economic needs of capitalism. As workers, most men in our culture (like working women) are controlled, dominated. Unlike working women, working men are fed daily a fantasy diet of male supremacy and power. In actuality, they have very little power, and they know it. Yet they do not rebel against the economic order or make revolution. They are socialized by ruling powers to accept their dehumanization and exploitation in the public world of work, and they are taught to expect that the private world, the world of home and intimate relationships, will restore to them their sense of power, which they equate with masculinity. They are taught that they will be able to rule in the home, to control and dominate, that this is the big payoff for their acceptance of an exploitative economic social order. By condoning and perpetuating male domination of women to prevent rebellion on the job, ruling male capitalists ensure that male violence will be expressed in the home and not in the work force.

The entry of women into the work force, which also serves the interests of capitalism, has taken even more control over women away from men. Therefore men rely more on the use of violence to establish and maintain a sex-role hierarchy in which they are in a dominant position. At one time, their dominance was determined by the fact that they were the sole wage earners. Their need to dominate women (socially constructed by the ideology of male supremacy), coupled with suppressed aggression towards employers who "rule" over them, makes the domestic environment the center of explosive tensions that lead to violence. Women are the targets because there is no fear that men will suffer or be severely punished if they hurt women, especially wives and lovers. They would be punished if they violently attacked employers, police officers.

Black women and men have always called attention to a "cycle of violence" that begins with psychological abuse in the public world wherein the male worker may be subjected to control by a boss or authority figure that is humiliating and degrading. Since he depends on the work situation for material survival, he does not strike out or oppose the employer who would punish him by taking his job or imprisoning him. He suppresses this violence and releases it in what I call a "control" situation, a situation where he has no need to fear retaliation, wherein he does not have to suffer as a consequence of acting violently. The home is usually this control situation, and the target for his abuse is usually female. Though his own expression of violence against women stems in part from the emotional pain he feels, the pain is released and projected onto the female. When the pain disappears he feels relief, even pleasure. His pain is gone even though it was not confronted or resolved in a healthy way. As the psychology of masculinity in sexist societies teaches men that to acknowledge and express pain negates masculinity and is a symbolic castration, causing pain rather than expressing it restores men's sense of completeness, of wholeness, of masculinity. The fate of many young black men in this society, whose lives are characterized by cycles of violence that usually climax in the death of others or their own deaths, epitomizes the peril of trying to actualize the fantasy of masculinity that is socially constructed by ruling groups in capitalist patriarchy.

Unlike many feminist activists writing about male violence against women, black women and men emphasize a "cycle of violence" that begins in the workplace because we are aware that systematic abuse is not confined to the domestic sphere, even though violent abuse is more commonly acted out in the home. To break out of this cycle of violence, to liberate themselves, black men and all men must begin to criticize the sexist notion of masculinity, to examine the impact of capitalism on their lives—the extent to which they feel degraded, alienated, and exploited in the work force. Men must begin to challenge notions of masculinity that equate manhood with ability to exert power over others, especially through the use of coercive force. Much of this work has to be done by men who are not violent, who have rejected the values of capitalist patriarchy. Most men who are violent against women are not seeking help or change. They do not feel that their acceptance and perpetration of violence against women is wrong. How can it be wrong if society rewards them for it? Television screens are literally flooded daily with tales of male violence, especially male violence against women. It is glamorized, made entertaining and sexually titillating. The more violent a male character is, whether he be hero or villain, the more attention he receives. Often a male hero has to exert harsher violence to subdue a villain. This violence is affirmed and rewarded. The more violent the male hero is (usually in his quest to save or protect a woman/victim), the more he receives love and affirmation from women. His acts of violence in the interest of protection are seen as a gesture of care, of his "love" for women and his concern for humanity.

This equation of violence with love on the part of women and men is another reason it is difficult to motivate most people to work to end violence. In real life, the equation of love with violence is part of early childhood socialization. An article in the October 1982 issue of *Mademoiselle* magazine, "A Special Report on Love, Violence, and the Single Woman," by Jane Patrick, calls attention to the fact that many women who are neither economically dependent on men nor bound to them through legal contracts do not reject males who are violent because they equate it with love. Patrick quotes Rodney Cate, professor of family studies, who links violence between parents and children to adult acceptance of violence in intimate relationships:

> When you examine the context in which parents suffer their chil-
> dren, it is easier to understand how the victim—and the
> abuser—equate the violence with love. It's not hard to see how
> over time we begin to pair some sort of physical punishment with
> love and to believe that someone is hurting us because they love us.

Many parents teach children that violence is the easiest way (if not the most acceptable way) to end a conflict and assert power. By saying things like "I'm only doing this because I love you" while they are using physical abuse to control children, parents are not only equating violence with love, they are also offering a notion of love synonymous with passive acceptance, the absence of explanation and discussions. In many homes small children and teenagers find their desire to discuss issues with parents sometimes viewed as a challenge to parental authority or power, as an act of "unlove." Force is used by the parent to meet this perceived challenge or threat. Again, it needs to be emphasized that the idea that it is correct to use abuse to maintain authority is taught to individuals by church, school, and other institutions.

Love and violence have become so intertwined in this society that many people, especially women, fear that eliminating violence will lead to the loss of love. Popular paperback romances, like the Harlequin series, which ten years ago had no descriptions of male violence against women, now describe acts of hitting, rape, etc., all in the context of romantic love. It is interesting to note that most women in these romances now have professional careers and are often sexually experienced. Male violence, the romances suggest, has to be used to subdue these "uppity" women who, though equal to men in the workplace, must be forced to assume a subordinate position in the home. There is little suggestion that women should stop working. Their work is depicted as a gesture of defiance that adds passion to the sexual conflict at home, heightening sexual pleasure when the male uses force to transform the "uppity" woman into a passive, submissive being. Of course, the man is always white, rich, and a member of the ruling class.

These romances are read by millions of women who spend millions of hard-earned dollars to read material that reinforces sexist role patterns and romanticizes violence against women. It should be noted that they also uphold white supremacy and Western imperialism. Women reading romances are being encouraged to accept the idea that violence heightens and intensifies sexual pleasure. They are also encouraged to believe that violence is a sign of masculinity and a gesture of male care, that the degree to which a man becomes violently angry corresponds to the intensity of his affection and care. Therefore, women readers learn that passive acceptance of violence is essential if they are to receive the rewards of love and care. This is often the case in women's lives. They may accept violence in intimate relationships, whether heterosexual or lesbian, because they do not wish to give up that care. They see enduring abuse as the price they pay. They know they can live without abuse; they do not think they can live without care.

Speaking of why poor women may not leave violent relationships, Schechter says, "Poor people experience so many different kinds of oppression, violence may be responded to as one of many abuses." Certainly many black women feel they must confront a degree of abuse wherever they turn in this society. Black women as well as many other marginalized groups in graduate schools are often psychologically abused by professors who systematically degrade and humiliate them for a period of years, as long as it takes for the woman to finish her degree or to be so "messed up" that she drops out. Black women in professional positions who appear to have "made it" are often the targets of abuse by employers and co-workers who resent their presence. Black women who work in service jobs are daily bombarded with belittling, degrading comments and gestures on the part of the people who have power over them. The vast majority of poor black women in this society find they are continually subjected to abuse in public agencies, stores, etc. These women often feel that abuse will be an element in most of their personal interactions. They are more inclined to accept abuse in situations where there are some rewards or benefits, where abuse is not the sole characteristic of the interaction. Since this is usually the case in situations where male violence occurs, they may be reluctant, even unwilling, to end these relationships. Like other groups of women, they fear the loss of care.

Until women and men cease equating violence with love, understand that disagreements and conflicts in the context of intimate relationships can be resolved without violence, and reject the idea that men should dominate women, male violence against women will continue, and so will other forms of violent aggression in intimate relationships. To help bring an end to violence against women, feminist activists have taken the lead in criticizing the ideology of male supremacy and showing the ways in which it supports and condones that violence. Yet efforts to end male violence against women will succeed only if they are part of an overall struggle to end violence.

Currently feminist activists supporting nuclear disarmament link militarism and patriarchy, showing connections between the two. Like analysis of violence against women, the tendency in these discussions is to focus on male support of violence—a focus that limits our understanding of the problem. Many women who advocate feminism see militarism as exemplifying patriarchal concepts of masculinity and the right of males to dominate others. To these women, to struggle against militarism is to struggle against patriarchy and male violence against women. Introducing a recently published book of essays, *Ain't Nowhere We Can Run: A Handbook for Women on the Nuclear Mentality*, Susan Koen writes:

> It is our belief that the tyranny created by nuclear activities is merely the latest and most serious manifestation of a culture characterized in every sphere by domination and exploitation. For this reason, the presence of the nuclear mentality in the world can only be viewed as one part of the whole, not an isolated issue. We urge the realization that separating the issue of nuclear power plants and weapons from the dominant cultural, social, and political perspectives of our society results in a limited understanding of the problem, and in turn limits the range of possible solutions. We offer then the argument that those male-defined constructs which control our social structures and relationships are directly responsible for the proliferation of nuclear plants and weapons. Patriarchy is the root of the problem, and the imminent dangers

created by the nuclear mentality serve to call our attention to the basic problem of patriarchy.

By equating militarism and patriarchy, women who advocate feminism often structure their arguments in such a way as to suggest that to be male is synonymous with strength, aggression, and the will to dominate and do violence to others; to be female is synonymous with weakness, passivity, and the will to nourish and affirm the lives of others. Such dualistic thinking is basic to all forms of social domination in Western society. Even when inverted and employed for a meaningful purpose such as nuclear disarmament, it is nevertheless dangerous because it reinforces the cultural basis of sexism and other forms of group oppression. It promotes a stereotypical notion of inherent differences between men and women, implying that women by virtue of their sex have played no crucial role in supporting and upholding imperialism (and the militarism that serves to maintain imperialist rule) or other systems of domination. Even if one argues that men have been taught to equate masculinity with the ability to do violence and women have been taught to equate femaleness with nurturance, the fact remains that many women and men do not conform to these stereotypes. Rather than clarifying for women the power we exert in the maintenance of systems of domination and setting forth strategies for resistance and change, most current discussion of feminism and militarism further mystifies women's role.

In keeping with the tenets of sexist ideology, women are talked about in these discussions as objects rather than subjects. We are depicted not as workers and activists, who, like men, make political choices, but as passive observers who have taken no responsibility for actively maintaining the value system of this society, which proclaims violence and domination the most effective tools of communication in human interaction, a value system that advocates and makes war. Discussions of feminism and militarism that do not clarify for women the roles we have played and play in all their variety and complexity make it appear that all women are against war and oppose the use of violence, and that men are the problem, the enemy. This is a distortion of women's experience, not a clarification of it or a redefinition. Devaluing the roles women have played necessarily leads to a distorted perspective on women's reality. I use the word "devaluing," for it seems that the suggestion that men have made war and war policy while women have passively watched represents a refusal to see women as active political beings even when we are subordinate to men. The assumption that to be deemed inferior or submissive necessarily defines what one actually is or how one actually behaves is a continuation of sexist patterns that deny the relative powers women have exercised. Even the woman who votes according to her husband's example is making a political choice. We need to see women as political beings.

An example of the distorted perception of women's reality that is being described by some activists who discuss women and militarism is the popular assumption that "women are natural enemies of war." Many female anti-war activists suggest that women as bearers of children, or the potential bearers of children, are necessarily more concerned about ending war than men—the implication being that women are more life-affirming. Leslie Cagan, in a recent interview in *South End Press News,* confirms that women participating in disarmament work often suggest that because they bear children, they have a "special relationship and responsibility to the survival of the planet." Cagan maintains that this is a "dangerous perspective" because it focuses on women's biology and "tends to reinforce the sexist notion that womanhood equals motherhood." She explains:

> It may be that some, even many, women are motivated to activism through concern for their children. It may also be a factor for some fathers who don't want to see their kids blown up in a nuclear war, either! But this simply doesn't justify a narrow and limiting perspective. It is limiting because it says that women's relationship to such an important issue as the future of our planet rests on a single biological fact.

We who are concerned about feminism and militarism must insist that women (even those who are bearers of children) are not inherently non-violent or life-affirming. Many women who mother (either as single parents or in camaraderie with husbands) have taught male children to see fighting and other forms of violent aggression as acceptable modes of communication, modes that are valued more than loving or caring interaction. Even though women often assume nurturing, life-affirming roles in their relationship to others, they do not necessarily value or respect that role as much as they revere the suppression of emotion or the assertion of power through the use of force. We must insist that women who do choose (even if they are inspired by motherhood) to denounce violence and domination and their ultimate expression, war, are political thinkers making political decisions and choices. If women who work against militarism continue to imply, however directly or indirectly, that there is an inherent predisposition in women to oppose war, they risk reinforcing the very biological determinism that is the philosophical foundation of notions of male supremacy. They also run the risk of covering up the reality that masses of women in the United States are not anti-imperialist, are not against militarism, and do not oppose the use of violence as a form of social control. Until these women change their values, they must be seen as clinging, like their male counterparts, to a perspective on human relationships that embraces social domination in all its various forms, and they must be held accountable for their actions.

Imperialism and not patriarchy is the core foundation of modern militarism (even though it serves the interest of imperialism to link notions of masculinity with the struggle to conquer nations and peoples). Many societies in the world that are ruled by males are not imperialistic; many women in the United States have made political decisions to support imperialism and militarism. Historically, white women in the United States working for women's rights have felt no contradiction between this effort and their support of the Western imperialist attempt to conquer the planet. Often they argued that equal rights would better enable white women to help in the building of this "great nation," i.e., in the cause of imperialism. Many white women in the early part of the twentieth century who were strong advocates of women's liberation were pro-imperialist.

Books like Helen Montgomery's *Western Women in Eastern Lands,* published in 1910, outlining fifty years of white women's work in foreign missions, document the link between the struggle for the emancipation of white women in the United States and the imperialist, hegemonic spread of Western values and Western domination of the globe. As missionaries, white women traveled to Eastern lands armed with psychological weapons that undermined the belief systems of Eastern women and replaced them with Western values. In the closing statement of her work, Helen Montgomery writes:

> So many voices are calling us, so many goods demand our allegiance, that we are in danger of forgetting the best. To seek first to bring Christ's kingdom on the earth, to respond to the need that is sorest, to go out into the desert for that loved and bewildered sheep that the shepherd has missed from the fold, to share all of the privilege with the unprivileged and happiness with the unhappy, to see the possibility of one redeemed earth, undivided, unvexed, unperplexed resting in the light of the glorious Gospel of the blessed God, this is the mission of the women's missionary movement.

Despite the fact that contemporary feminist movement against imperialism and militarism is headed by white women, they are a small minority and do not represent the values of the majority of white women in this society or of women as a whole. Many white women in the United States continue to wholeheartedly support militarism. Feminist activists must hold these women accountable for their political decisions and must also work to change their perspectives. We avoid this challenge when we act as if men and patriarchy are the sole evils.

It is a quite blatant truth that men commit the majority of imperialist acts globally, that men have committed the majority of violent acts in war. However, we must remember that when called to do so in times of national crisis, women fight in combat and are not necessarily opposed to war. We must also remember that war does not simply include fighting and that women's effort on the home front and off the front lines has helped make war. At the end of her essay discussing women's participation in war effort, "The Culture in Our Blood," Patty Walton writes:

> Women have not fought in wars because of our material circumstances and not because we are innately more moral than men or because of any biological limitation on our part. The work of women supports both a society's war and its peace activities. And our support has always derived from our particular socialization as women. In fact, the socialization of women and men complements the needs of the culture in which we live. It is necessary to recognize this because we need to change these material relationships and not just the sex of our world problem-makers. Men are not more innately aggressive than women are passive. We have cultures of war, so we can have cultures of peace.

Sex-role divisions of labor have meant that as parents women have supported war effort by instilling in their children an acceptance of domination and a respect for violence as a means of social control. Implanting this ideology in human consciousness is as central to the making of a militaristic state as the overall control of males by ruling male groups who insist that men make war, and reward them for their efforts. Like men, women in the United States have a high tolerance for witnessing violence, learned through excessive television-watching. To fight militarism, we must resist the socialization and brainwashing that teaches passive acceptance of violence in daily life, that tells us violence can be eliminated with violence. Women who are against militarism must withdraw support for war by working to transform passive acceptance of violence as a means of social control in everyday life.

This means that we must no longer act as if men are the only people who act violently, who accept and condone violence, who create a culture of violence. As women we must assume responsibility for the role women play in condoning violence. By only calling attention to male violence against women, or making militarism just another expression of male violence, we fail to adequately address the problem of violence and make it difficult to develop viable resistance strategies and solutions. (A fuller discussion of the impact of militarism on women's lives may be found in Cynthia Enloe's work *Does Khaki Become You?*) While we need not diminish the severity of the problem of male violence against women or male violence against nations or the planet, we must acknowledge that men and women have together made the United States a culture of violence and must work together to transform and recreate that culture. Women and men must oppose the use of violence as a means of social control in all its manifestations: war, male violence against women, adult violence against children, teenage violence, racial violence, etc. Feminist efforts to end male violence against women must be expanded into a movement to end all forms of violence. Broadly based, such a movement could potentially radicalize consciousness and intensify awareness of the need to end male domination of women in a context in which we are working to eradicate the idea that hierarchical structures should be the basis of human interaction.

10

REVOLUTIONARY
PARENTING

During the early stages of contemporary women's liberation movement, feminist analyses of motherhood reflected the race and class
biases of participants. Some white, middle-class, college-educated
women argued that motherhood was a serious obstacle to women's
liberation, a trap confining women to the home, keeping them tied
to cleaning, cooking, and child care. Others simply identified motherhood and child-rearing as the locus of women's oppression. Had
black women voiced their views on motherhood, it would not have
been named a serious obstacle to our freedom as women. Racism,
lack of jobs, lack of skills or education, and a number of other issues
would have been at the top of the list—but not motherhood. Black
women would not have said motherhood prevented us from enter-
ing the world of paid work because we have always worked. From
slavery to the present day, black women in the U.S. have worked
outside the home, in the fields, in the factories, in the laundries, in
the homes of others. That work gave meager financial compensa-
tion and often interfered with or prevented effective parenting. Historically, black women have identified work in the context of family
as humanizing labor, work that affirms their identity as women, as
human beings showing love and care, the very gestures of humanity
white supremacist ideology claimed black people were incapable of
expressing. In contrast to labor done in a caring environment inside

the home, labor outside the home was most often seen as stressful, degrading, and dehumanizing.

These views on motherhood and work outside the home contrasted sharply with those expressed by white women's liberationists. Many black women were saying, "We want to have more time to share with family, we want to leave the world of alienated work." Many white women's liberationists were saying, "We are tired of the isolation of the home, tired of relating only to children and husband, tired of being emotionally and economically dependent; we want to be liberated to enter the world of work." (These voices were not those of working-class white women who were, like black women workers, tired of alienated labor.) The women's liberationists who wanted to enter the work force did not see this world as a world of alienated work. They do now. In the last twenty years of feminist movement, many middle-class white women have entered the wage-earning work force and have found that working within a social context where sexism is still the norm, where there is unnecessary competition promoting envy, distrust, antagonism, and malice between individuals, makes work stressful, frustrating, and often totally unsatisfying. Concurrently, many women who like and enjoy the wage work they do feel that it takes too much of their time, leaving little space for other satisfying pursuits. While work may help women gain a degree of financial independence or even financial self-sufficiency, for most women it has not adequately fulfilled human needs. As a consequence, women's search for fulfilling labor done in an environment of care has led to reemphasizing the importance of family and the positive aspects of motherhood. Additionally, the fact that many active feminists are in their mid- to late-thirties, facing the biological clock, has focused collective attention on motherhood. This renewed attention has led many women active in the feminist movement who were interested in child-rearing to choose to bear children.

Although early feminists demanded respect and acknowledgment for housework and child care, they did not attribute enough significance and value to female parenting, to motherhood. It is a gesture that should have been made at the onset of feminist movement. Early feminist attacks on motherhood alienated masses of women from the movement, especially poor and/or non-white women, who find parenting one of the few interpersonal relationships where they are affirmed and appreciated. Unfortunately, recent positive feminist focus on motherhood draws heavily on sexist stereotypes. Motherhood is as romanticized by some feminist activists as it was by the nineteenth-century men and women who extolled the virtues of the "cult of domesticity." The one significant difference in their approach is that motherhood is no longer viewed as taking place primarily within the framework of heterosexual marriage or even heterosexual relationships. More than ever before, women who are not attached to males, who may be heterosexual or lesbian, are choosing to bear children. In spite of the difficulties (especially economic) of single parenting in this society, the focus is on "joys of motherhood," the special intimacy, closeness, and bonding purported to characterize the mother/child relationship. Books like Phyllis Chesler's *With Child: A Diary of Motherhood* rhapsodize over the pleasures and joys of childbirth and child care. Publication of more scholarly and serious works like Jessie Bernard's *The Future of Motherhood,* Elisabeth Badinter's *Mother Love,* Nancy Friday's *My Mother/My Self,* and Nancy Chodorow's *The Reproduction of Mothering* reflect growing concern with motherhood.

This resurgence of interest in motherhood has positive and negative implications for feminist movement. On the positive side there is a continual need for study and research of female parenting, which this interest promotes and encourages. In the foreword to *Of Woman Born,* Adrienne Rich states that she felt it was important to write a book on motherhood because it is "a crucial, still relatively unexplored area for feminist theory." It is also positive that women who choose to bear children need no longer fear that this choice excludes them from recognition by feminist movement, although it may still exclude them from active participation. On the negative side, romanticizing motherhood, employing the same terminology that is used by sexists to suggest that women are inherently life-affirming nurturers, feminist activists reinforce central tenets of male supremacist ideology. They imply that motherhood is a woman's truest vocation; that women who do not mother, whose lives may be focused more exclusively on a career, creative work, or political work, are missing out, are doomed to live emotionally unfulfilled lives. While they do not openly attack or denigrate women who do not bear children, they (like the society as a whole) suggest that it is *more* important than women's other labor and more rewarding. They could simply state that it *is* important and rewarding. Significantly, this perspective is often voiced by many of the white bourgeois women with successful careers who are now choosing to bear children. They seem to be saying to masses of women that careers or work can never be as important, as satisfying, as bearing children.

This is an especially dangerous line of thinking, coming at a time when teenage women who have not realized a number of goals are bearing children in large numbers rather than postponing parenting, when masses of women are being told by the government that they are destroying family life by not assuming sexist-defined roles. Through mass media and other communication systems, women are currently inundated with material encouraging them to bear children. Newspapers carry headline stories with titles like "Motherhood is making a comeback"; women's magazines are flooded with articles on the new motherhood; fashion magazines have special features on designer clothing for the pregnant woman; television talk shows do special features on career women who are now choosing to raise children. Coming at a time when women with children are more likely to live in poverty, when the number of homeless, parentless children increases by the thousands daily, when women continue to assume sole responsibility for parenting, such propaganda undermines and threatens feminist movement.

To some extent, the romanticization of motherhood by bourgeois white women is an attempt to repair the damage done by past feminist critiques and give women who mother the respect they deserve. It should be noted that even the most outrageous of these criticisms did not compare with sexism as a source of exploitation and humiliation for mothers. Female parenting is significant and valuable work which must be recognized as such by everyone in society, including feminist activists. It should receive deserved recognition, praise, and celebration within a feminist context where there is renewed effort to rethink the nature of motherhood; to make motherhood neither a compulsory experience for women nor an exploitative or oppressive one; to make female parenting good, effective parenting whether it is done exclusively by women or in conjunction with men.

In a recent article, "Bringing Up Baby," Mary Ellen Schoonmaker stressed the often-made point that men do not share equally in parenting:

> Since the early days of ambivalence toward motherhood, the overall goal of the women's movement has been a quest for equality—to take the oppression out of mothering, to join "mothering" to "parenting," and for those who choose to have children to share parenting with men and with society in general. Looking back over the past twenty years, it seems as if these goals have been among the hardest for the women's movement to reach.
>
> If men did equally share in parenting, it would mean trading places with women part of the time. Many men have found it easier to share power with women on the job than they have in the home. Even though millions of mothers with infants and toddlers now work outside the home, many women still do the bulk of the housework.

Men will not share equally in parenting until they are taught, ideally from childhood on, that fatherhood has the same meaning and significance as motherhood. As long as women or society as a whole see the mother/child relationship as unique and special because the female carries the child in her body and gives birth, or makes this biological experience synonymous with women having a closer, more significant bond to children than the male parent, responsibility for child care and child-rearing will continue to be primarily women's work. Even the childless woman is considered more suited to raise children than the male parent because she is seen as an inherently caring nurturer. The biological experience of pregnancy and childbirth, whether painful or joyful, should not be equated with the idea that women's parenting is necessarily superior to men's.

Dictionary definitions of the word "father" relate its meaning to accepting responsibility, with no mention of words like "tenderness" and "affection," yet these words are used to define what the word "mother" means. By placing sole responsibility for nurturing—that is to say for satisfying the emotional and material needs of children—onto women, society reinforces the notion that to mother is more important than to father. Structured into the definitions and the very usage of the terms "father" and "mother" is the sense that these two words refer to two distinctly different experiences. Women and men must define the work of fathering and mothering in the same way if males and females are to accept equal responsibility in parenting. Even feminist theorists who have emphasized the need for men to share equally in child-rearing are reluctant to cease attaching special value to mothering. This illustrates feminists' willingness to glorify the physiological experience of motherhood, as well as unwillingness to concede motherhood as an arena of social life in which women can exert power and control.

Women and society as a whole often consider the father who does equal parenting unique and special rather than as representative of what should be the norm. Such a man may even be seen as assuming a "maternal" role. Describing men who parent in her work *Mother Love,* Elisabeth Badinter comments:

> Under the pressure exerted by women, the new father mothers equally and in the traditional mother's image. He creeps in, like another mother, between the mother and the child, who experiences almost indiscriminately as intimate a contact with the father as with the mother. We have only to notice the increasingly numerous photographs in magazines showing fathers pressing newborns against their bare chests. Their faces reflect a completely motherly tenderness that shocks no one. After centuries of the father's authority or absence, it seems that a new concept has come into existence—father love, the exact equivalent of mother love. While it is obvious that women who parent would necessarily be the models men would strive to emulate (since women have been doing effective parenting for many more years), these men are becoming parents, effective fathers. They are not becoming mothers.

Another example of this tendency occurs at the end of Sara Ruddick's essay "Maternal Thinking." She envisions a time in which men will share equally in child-rearing and writes:

> On that day there will be no more "fathers," no more people of either sex who have power over their children's lives and moral authority in their children's worlds, though they do the work of attentive love. There will be mothers of both sexes who live out a transformed maternal thought in communities that share parental care—practically, emotionally, economically, and socially. Such communities will have learned from their mothers how to value children's lives.

In this paragraph, as in the entire essay, Ruddick romanticizes the idea of the "maternal" and places emphasis on men becoming maternal, a vision that seems shortsighted. Because the word "maternal" is associated with the behavior of women, men will not identify with it even though they may be behaving in ways that have traditionally been seen as "feminine." Wishful thinking will not alter the concept of the maternal in our society. Rather than changing it, the word "paternal" should share the same meaning. Telling a boy acting out the role of caring parent with his dolls that he is being maternal will not change the idea that women are better suited to parenting; it will reinforce it. Saying to a boy that he is behaving like a good father (in the way that girls are told that they are good mothers when they show attention and care to dolls) would teach him a vision of effective parenting, of fatherhood, that is the same as motherhood.

Seeing men who do effective parenting as "maternal" reinforces the stereotypical sexist notion that women are inherently better suited to parent, that men who parent in the same way as women are imitating the real thing rather than acting as a parent should act. There should be a concept of effective parenting that makes no distinction between maternal and paternal care. The model of effective parenting that includes the kind of attentive love Ruddick describes has been applied only to women and has prevented fathers from learning how to parent. They are allowed to conceive of the father's role solely in terms of exercising authority and providing for mate-

rial needs. They are taught to think of it as a role secondary to the
mother's. Until males are taught how to parent using the same
model of effective parenting that has been taught to women, they
will not participate equally in child care. They will even feel that they
should not participate because they have been taught to think they
are inadequate or ineffective child-rearers.

Men are socialized to avoid assuming responsibility for
child-rearing, and that avoidance is supported by women who believe that motherhood is a sphere of power they would lose if men
participated equally in parenting. Many of these women do not wish
to share parenting equally with men. In feminist circles it is often
forgotten that masses of women in the United States still believe
that men cannot parent effectively and should not even attempt to
parent. Until these women understand that men should and can do
primary parenting, they will not expect the men in their lives to share
equally in child-rearing. Even when they do, it is unlikely that men
will respond with enthusiasm. People need to know the negative impact that male non-participation in child-rearing has on family relationships and child development.

Feminist efforts to point out to men what they lose when they
do not participate in parenting tend to be directed at the bourgeois
classes. Little is done to discuss non-sexist parenting or male
parenting with poor and working-class women and men. In fact, the
kind of maternal care Ruddick evokes in her essay, with its tremendous emphasis on attention given children by parents, especially
mothers, is a form of parental care that is difficult for many
working-class parents to offer when they return home from work
tired and exhausted. It is increasingly difficult for women and men
in families struggling to survive economically to give special attention
to parenting. Their struggle contrasts sharply with the family structure of the bourgeoisie. Their white women and men are likely to be
better informed about the positive effects of male participation in
parenting, to have more time to parent, and not to be perpetually
anxious about their material well-being. It is also difficult for women
who parent alone to juggle the demands of work and child-rearing.

Feminist theorists point to the problems that arise when

parenting is done exclusively by an individual or solely by women: female parenting gives children few role models of male parenting, perpetuates the idea that parenting is a woman's vocation, and reinforces male domination and fear of women. Society, however, is not concerned. This information has little impact at a time when men, more than ever before, avoid responsibility for child-rearing, and when women are parenting less because they work more but are parenting more often alone. These facts raise two issues that must be of central concern for future feminist movement: the right of children to effective child care by parents and other child-rearers, and the restructuring of society so that women do not exclusively provide that care.

Eliminating sexism is the solution to the problem of men participating unequally or not at all in child care. Therefore more women and men must recognize the need to support and participate in feminist movement. Masses of women continue to believe that they should be primarily responsible for child care—this point cannot be overemphasized. Feminist efforts to help women unlearn this socialization could lead to greater demands on their part for men to participate equally in parenting. Making and distributing brochures in women's health centers and in other public places that would emphasize the importance of males and females sharing equally in parenting is one way to make more people aware of this need. Seminars on parenting that emphasize non-sexist parenting and joint parenting by women and men in local communities is another way more people could learn about the subject. Before women become pregnant, they need to understand the significance of men sharing equally in parenting. Some women in relationships with men, who may be considering bearing children, do not do so because male partners make it known that they will not assume responsibility for parenting. These women feel their decision not to bear children with men who refuse to share parenting is a political statement reinforcing the importance of equal participation in parenting and the need to end male dominance of women. We need to hear more from these women about the choices they have made. There are also women who bear children in relationships with men who know beforehand that the man will not participate equally in parenting. It is important for future studies of female parenting to understand their choices.

Women need to know that it is important to discuss child care with men before children are conceived or born. There are women and men who have made either legal contracts or simply written agreements that spell out each individual's responsibility. Some women have found that men verbally support the idea of shared parenting before a child is conceived or born and then do not follow through. Written agreements can help clarify the situation by requiring each individual to discuss what they feel about parental care, who should be responsible, etc. Most women and men do not discuss the nature of child-rearing before children are born because it is simply assumed that women will be caretakers.

Despite the importance of men sharing equally in parenting, large numbers of women have no relationship to the man with whom they have conceived a child. In some cases, this is a reflection of the man's lack of concern about parenting or the woman's choice. Some women do not feel it is important for their children to experience caring, nurturing parenting from males. In black communities, it is not unusual for a single female parent to rely on male relatives and friends to help with child-rearing. As more heterosexual and lesbian women choose to bear children with no firm ties to male parents, there will exist a greater need for community-based child care that would bring children into contact with male child-rearers so they will not grow to maturity thinking women are the only group that does or should do child-rearing. The child-rearer does not have to be a parent. Child-rearers in our culture are teachers, librarians, etc., and even though these are occupations that have been dominated by women, this is changing. In these contexts, a child could experience male child-rearing. Some female parents who raise their children without the mutual care of fathers feel their own positions are undermined when they meet occasionally with male parents who may provide a good time but be totally unengaged in day-to-day parenting. They sometimes have to cope with children valuing the male parent more because he is male (and sexist ideology teaches them that his attentions are more valuable than female care). These women need to know that teaching their children non-sexist values could help them appreciate female parenting and could eradicate favoritism based solely on sexist standards.

Because women are doing most of the parenting, the need for tax-funded public child-care centers with equal numbers of non-sexist male and female workers continues to be a pressing feminist issue. Such centers would relieve individual women of the sole responsibility for child-rearing as well as help promote awareness of the necessity for male participation in child-raising. Yet this is an issue that has yet to be pushed by masses of people. Future feminist organizing (especially in the interests of building mass-based feminist movement) could use this issue as a platform. Feminist activists have always seen public child care as one solution to the problem of women being the primary child-rearers. Commenting on the need for child-care centers in her article "Bringing Up Baby," Schoonmaker writes:

> As for child care outside the home, the seemingly simple concept envisioned by the women's movement of accessible, reliable, quality day care has proven largely elusive. While private, often overpriced sources of day care have risen to meet middle-class needs, the inadequacy of public day care remains an outrage. The Children's Defense Fund, a child advocacy and lobbying group in Washington, D.C., reports that perhaps six to seven million children, including preschoolers, may be left at home alone while their parents work because they can't afford day care.

Most child-care centers, catering either to the needs of the working classes or the bourgeoisie, are not non-sexist. Until children begin to learn at a very early age that it is not important to make role distinctions based on sex, they will continue to grow to maturity thinking that women should be the primary child-rearers.

Many people oppose the idea of tax-funded public child care because they see it as an attempt by women to avoid parenting. They need to know that the isolated parenting that women do in this society is not the best way to raise children or treat women who mother. Elizabeth Janeway makes this point in her book *Cross Sections*, emphasizing that the idea of an individual having sole responsibility for child-rearing is the most unusual pattern of parenting in the world, one that has proved to be unsuccessful because it isolates children and parents from society:

> How extreme that family isolation can be today is indicated by these instances listed in a study undertaken for the Massachusetts Advisory Council on Education.... This group found:
>
> 1. Isolation of wage earners from spouses and children, caused by the wage earners' absorption into the world of work.
>
> 2. The complementary isolation of young children from the occupational world of parents and other adults.
>
> 3. The general isolation of young children from persons of different ages, both adults and other children.
>
> 4. The residential isolation of families from persons of different social, ethnic, religious, and racial backgrounds.
>
> 5. The isolation of family members from kin and neighbors.
>
> Such isolation means that the role of the family as the agent for socializing children is inadequately fulfilled at present whether or not mothers are at work outside the home. Children are now growing up without the benefit of a variety of adult role models of both sexes and in ignorance of the world of paid work. Returning women to a life centered in home and family would not solve the fundamental loss of connection between family and community. The effort by the women's movement to see that centers for child care are provided by society is not an attempt to hand over to others the duties of motherhood but to enlist community aid to supplement the proper obligations of parents, as was often the practice in the past.

Small, community-based, public child-care centers would be the best way to overcome this isolation. When parents must drive long distances to take children to day care, dependency on parents is increased and not lessened. Community-based, public child-care centers would give small children great control over their lives.

Child care is a responsibility that can be shared with other child-rearers, with people who do not live with children. This form of parenting is revolutionary in this society because it takes place in opposition to the idea that parents, especially mothers, should be the only child-rearers. Many people raised in black communities experienced this type of community-based child care. Black women who had to leave the home and work to help provide for families could not afford to send children to day-care centers, and such centers did not always exist. They relied on people in their communities to help. Even in families where the mother stayed home, she could also rely on people in the community to help. She did not need to go with her children every time they walked to the playground to watch them because they would be watched by a number of people living near the playground. People who did not have children often took responsibility for sharing in child-rearing. In my own family, there were seven children, and when we were growing up it was not possible for our parents to watch us all the time or even give that extra-special individual attention children sometimes desire. Those needs were often met by neighbors and people in the community.

This kind of shared responsibility for child care can happen in small community settings where people know and trust one another. It cannot happen in those settings if parents regard children as their "property," their "possessions." Many parents do not want their children to develop caring relationships with others, not even relatives. If there were community-based day-care centers, there would be a much greater likelihood that children would develop ongoing friendships and caring relationships with adult people other than their parents. These types of relationships are not formed in day-care centers where one teacher takes care of a large number of students, where one never sees teachers in any context other than school. Any individual who has been raised in an environment of communal child care knows that this happens only if parents can accept other adults assuming parental-type care for their children. While it creates a situation where children must respect a number of caretakers, it also gives children resources to rely on if their emotional, intellectual, and material needs are not met solely by parents. Often in black communities where shared child-rearing happens, elderly women and men participate. Today many children have no contact with the elderly. Another hazard of single parenting or even nuclear-family parenting that is avoided when there is community-based child-raising is the tendency of parents to overinvest emotion in their children. This is a problem for many people who choose to have children after years of thinking they would not. They may make children into "love objects" and have no interest in teaching them to relate to a wide variety of people. This is as much a problem for feminist women and men who are raising children as it is for other parents.

Initially, women's liberationists felt that the need for population control coupled with awareness of this society's consumption of much of the world's resources were political reasons not to bear children. These reasons have not changed even though they are now ignored or dismissed. Yet if there were less emphasis on having one's "own" children and more emphasis on raising children who are already living and in need of child care, there would be large groups of responsible women and men to share in the process of child-rearing. Lucia Valeska supported this position in an essay published in a 1975 issue of *Quest,* "If All Else Fails, I'm Still a Mother":

> To have our own biological children today is personally and politically irresponsible. If you have health, strength, energy, and financial assets to give to children, then do so. Who, then, will have children? If the childfree raise existing children, more people than ever will "have" children. The line between biological and nonbiological mothers will begin to disappear. Are we in danger of depleting the population? Are you kidding?
>
> Right now in your community there are hundreds of thousands of children and mothers who desperately need individual and community support.

Some people who choose not to bear children make an effort to participate in child-rearing. Yet, like many parents, most people without children assume they should be uninterested in child care until they have their "own" children. People without children who try to participate in child-rearing must confront the suspicions and resistance of people who do not understand their interest, who assume that all people without children do not like them. People are especially wary of individuals who wish to help in child-rearing if they do not ask for pay for their services. At a time in my life when my companion and I were working hard to participate in child-rearing we had children stay with us in our home for short periods of time to give the parent, usually a single mother, a break and to have children in our lives. If we explained the principle behind our actions, people were usually surprised and supportive, but wary. I think they were wary because our actions were unusual. The difficulties we faced have led us to accept a life in which we have less interaction with children than we would like, the case for most people who do not have children. This isolation from children has motivated many feminists to bear children.

Before there can be shared responsibility for child-rearing that relieves women of the sole responsibility for primary child care, women and men must revolutionize their consciousness. They must be willing to accept that parenting in isolation (irrespective of the sex of the parent) is not the most effective way to raise children or be happy as parents. Since women do most of the parenting in this society, and it does not appear that this situation will alter in the coming years, there has to be renewed feminist organizing around the issue of child care. The point is not to stigmatize single parents, but to emphasize the need for collective parenting. Women all over the United States must rally together to demand that tax money spent on the arms race and other militaristic goals be spent on improving the quality of parenting and child care in this society. Feminist theorists who emphasize the hazards of single parenting, who outline the need for men to share equally in parenting, often live in families where the male parent is present. This leads them to ignore the fact that this type of parenting is not an option for many women (even though it may be the best social framework in which to raise children). That social framework could be made available in community-based, public day-care centers with men and women sharing equal responsibility for child care. More than ever before, there is a great need for women and men to organize around the issue of child care to ensure that all children will be raised in the best possible social frameworks, to ensure that women will not be the sole, or primary, child-rearers.

ENDING FEMALE
SEXUAL OPPRESSION

During the early stages of contemporary feminist movement, women's liberation was often equated with sexual liberation. On the cover of Germaine Greer's *The Female Eunuch* (one of the most widely read feminist works in the '70s), the book is described as "the ultimate word on sexual freedom." On the back cover, Greer is described as "a woman with a sense of humor who is proud of her sexuality." (Germaine Greer's work *Sex and Destiny* is an interesting rethinking of the politics of fertility that challenges many notions of sexual freedom for women advocated by the author in her earlier work.) Feminist thinkers like Greer believed that assertion of the primacy of sexuality would be a liberatory gesture. They urged women to initiate sexual advances, to enjoy sex, to experiment with new relationships, to be sexually "free." Yet most women did not have the leisure, the mobility, the contacts, or even the desire to indulge in this so-called "sexual liberation." Young heterosexual women, single and childless; teenagers and college students; and political progressives were the groups most eager and able to pattern their sexual behavior after what was essentially an inversion of the male notion of sexual liberation. Advocating genuine sexual liberty was positive, and women learned from experience that the freedom to initiate sexual relationships; to be non-monogamous; to experiment with group sex, sexualized sado-masochism, etc. could sometimes be exciting and pleasurable; it did not, however, deconstruct the power relations between men and women in the sexual sphere. Many women felt disillusioned with the idea of sexual liberation. While some participants in feminist circles continued to emphasize the importance of sexual freedom, rejecting the idea that it should be patterned after a male model, a larger contingent, heterosexual and lesbian, began to denounce the idea of sexual freedom and even of sexual contact with men because they felt women were still exploited by the old sexual paradigms. Increasingly, these feminists came to see male sexuality as disgusting and necessarily exploitive of women.

Whether or not sexual freedom should be a feminist issue is currently a much-debated topic. (Since the writing of this chapter much new feminist writing discussing sexuality has emerged, including *Loving in the War Years,* by Cherríe Moraga; *Powers of Desire,* edited by Ann Snitow, Christine Stansell, and Sharon Thompson; *Female Desire,* by Rosalind Coward; and *Sex and Love,* edited by Sue Cartledge and Joanna Ryan; to name a few.) Concluding her essay "Sexuality as the Mainstay of Identity: Psychoanalytic Perspectives," Ethel Person writes:

> In sum, then, sexual liberation, while important and even crucial to some individuals, has significant limitations as social critique and political policy. At its worst, sexual liberation is part of the cult of individuality which only demands legitimation of the expression of the individual's need, what appears to be her raw "impulse" life, against the demands of society without considering a political reordering of the social order itself. The achievement of the conditions necessary to female autonomy is a precondition for authentic sexual liberation.

Person does not add that rethinking sexuality, changing the norms of sexuality, is a pre-condition for female sexual autonomy; therefore sexuality, and by implication "sexual freedom," is an important, relevant issue for feminist politics.

It has been a simple task for women to describe and criticize negative aspects of sexuality as it has been socially constructed in sexist society; to expose male objectification and dehumanization of women; to denounce rape, pornography, sexualized violence, incest, etc. It has been a far more difficult task for women to envision new sexual paradigms, to change the norms of sexuality. The inspiration for such work can only emerge in an environment where sexual well-being is valued. Ironically, some feminists have tended to dismiss issues of sexual pleasure, well-being, and contentedness as irrelevant. Contemporary emphasis on sexual revolution or anything-goes sexual expression has led many women and men to assume that sexual freedom already exists and is even overvalued in our society. However, this is *not* a culture that affirms real sexual freedom. Criticizing the assumption that this is a sexually liberated society because there is an absence of many restrictions, Ellen Willis asserts in her essay "Toward a Feminist Sexual Revolution":

> From a radical standpoint, then, sexual liberation involves not only the abolition of restrictions but the positive presence of social and psychological conditions that foster satisfying sexual relations. And from that standpoint, this culture is still deeply repressive. Most obviously, sexual inequality and the resulting antagonism between men and women constitute a devastating barrier to sexual happiness. I will argue in addition that, sexual liberalism notwithstanding, most children's upbringing produces adults with profoundly negative attitudes towards sex. Under these conditions, the relaxation of sexual restrictions leads people to try desperately to overcome the obstacles to satisfaction through compulsive sexual activity and preoccupation with sex. The emphasis on sex that currently permeates our public life—especially the enormous demands for sexual advice and therapy—attest not to our sexual freedom but to our continuing sexual frustration.

Feminist activists who see male sexuality as inherently despicable have been those most willing to de-emphasize issues of sexual freedom. Focusing solely on those aspects of male sexual expression that have to do with reinforcing male domination of women, they are reluctant and downright unwilling to acknowledge that sexuality as it is constructed in sexist society is no more "liberating" for men than it is for women (even though it is obviously oppressive to women in ways that are not oppressive to men). Willis argues that recognition of "sexual destructiveness can be seen as a perversion that both reflects and perpetuates a repressive system" so that it is possible "to envision a coherent feminist politics in which a commitment to sexual freedom plays an integral part." Sexual freedom can exist only when individuals are no longer oppressed by a socially constructed sexuality based on biologically determined definitions of sexuality: repression, guilt, shame, dominance, conquest, and exploitation. To set the stage for the development of that sexual freedom, feminist movement must continue to focus on ending female sexual oppression.

The focus on "sexual liberation" has always carried with it the assumption that the goal of such effort is to make it possible for individuals to engage in more and/or better sexual activity. Yet one aspect of sexual norms that many people find oppressive is the assumption that one "should" be engaged in sexual activity. This "should" is one expression of sexual coercion. Advocates of sexual liberation often imply that any individual who is not concerned about the quality of their experience or exercising greater sexual freedom is mentally disturbed or sexually repressed. When primary emphasis is placed on ending sexual oppression rather than on sexual liberation, it is possible to envision a society in which it is as much an expression of sexual freedom to choose not to participate in sexual activity as it is to choose to participate.

Sexual norms as they are currently socially constructed have always privileged active sexual expression over sexual desire. To act sexually is deemed natural, normal; to not act, unnatural, abnormal. Such thinking corresponds with sexist role patterning. Men are socialized to act sexually, women not to act (or to simply react to male sexual advances). Women's liberationists' insistence that women should be sexually active as a gesture of liberation helped free female sexuality from the restraints imposed upon it by repressive double standards, but it did not remove the stigma attached to sexual inactivity. Until that stigma is removed, women and men will not feel free to participate in sexual activity when they desire. They will continue to respond to coercion, either the sexist coercion that pushes young men to act sexually to prove their "masculinity" (i.e., their heterosexuality) or the sexual coercion that compels young women to respond to such advances to prove their "femininity" (i.e., their willingness to be heterosexual sex objects). The removal of the social stigma attached to sexual inactivity would amount to a change in sexual norms. It would have many positive implications for women and men, especially teenagers, who are at this historical moment most likely to be victimized by sexist sexual norms. Recent focus on sex between heterosexual teenagers indicates that coercion remains a central motivation for participation in sexual activity. Girls "do it for the boy," as one seventeen-year-old daughter told her mother (quoted in Ellen Goodman's essay "The Turmoil of Teenage Sexuality"), and boys do it to prove to other boys that they are heterosexual and that they can exert "masculine" power over girls.

Feminist movement to eradicate heterosexism—compulsory heterosexuality—is central to efforts to end sexual oppression. In the introduction to *No Turning Back: Lesbian and Gay Liberation of the '80s,* Gerre Goodman, George Lakey, Judy Lakey, and Erika Thorne define heterosexism as the:

> suppression and denial of homosexuality with the assumption that everyone is or should be heterosexual and, second, a belief in the inherent superiority of the dominant-male/passive-female role pattern. Heterosexism results in compulsory heterosexuality which cripples the free expression and mutually supportive relationships of heterosexuals as well as of lesbians and gay men.

Within the feminist movement lesbian women have worked hardest to call attention to the struggle to end heterosexist oppression. Lesbians have been on both sides of the larger sexual-liberation debate. They have shown many heterosexual women that their prejudices against lesbians support and perpetuate compulsory heterosexuality. They have also shown women that we can find emotional and mutual sexual fulfillment in relationships with one another. Some lesbians have suggested that homosexuality may be the most direct expression of pro-sex politics, since it is unconnected to procreation. Feminist movement to end female sexual oppression is linked to lesbian liberation. The struggle to end prejudice, exploitation, and oppression of lesbians and gay men is a crucial feminist agenda. It is a necessary component of the movement to end female sexual oppression. Affirming lesbianism, women of varied sexual preferences resist the perpetuation of compulsory heterosexuality.

Throughout feminist movement, there has been a tendency to make the struggle to end sexual oppression a competition: heterosexuality versus lesbianism. Early in the movement, attempts to exclude and silence lesbians were justified through the specter of a "lavender menace." Later, lesbianism was presented as a choice that would eliminate the need to deal with issues of heterosexual conflict or as the most politically correct choice for a feminist woman. Even though many feminists acknowledge that fighting sexual oppression, particularly male domination of women, is not the same as man-hating, within feminist gatherings and organizations intense anti-male sentiments are sometimes expressed by heterosexual women and lesbians alike, and women who are not lesbians, who may or may not be in relationships with men, feel that they are not "real" feminists. This is especially true of women who may support feminism but who do not publicly support lesbian rights. It is often forgotten that we are all in the process of developing radical political consciousness, that it is a "process," and that it defeats efforts to build solidarity to condemn or judge women politically incorrect when they do not immediately support all the issues we deem relevant.

The suggestion that the truly feminist woman is lesbian (made by heterosexuals and lesbians alike) sets up another sexual standard by which women are to be judged and found wanting. Although it is not common for women in the feminist movement to state that women should be lesbian, the message is transmitted via discussions of heterosexuality that suggest all genital contact between women and men is rape, that the woman who is emotionally and sexually committed to an individual man is necessarily incapable of loyal, woman-identified political commitment. Just as the struggle to end sexual oppression aims to eliminate heterosexism, it should not endorse any one sexual choice: celibacy, bisexuality, homosexuality, or heterosexuality. Feminist activists need to remember that the political choices we make are not determined by whom we choose to have genital sexual contact with. In her introduction to *Home Girls: A Black Feminist Anthology*, Barbara Smith asserts: "Black feminism and Black Lesbianism are not interchangeable. Feminism is a political movement, and many Lesbians are not feminists." This is also true for many heterosexual women. It is important for women, especially those who are heterosexual, to know that they can make a radical political commitment to feminist struggle even though they are sexually involved with men (many of us know from experience that political choice will undoubtedly alter the nature of individual relationships). All women need to know that they can be politically committed to feminism regardless of their sexual preference. They need to know that the goal of feminist movement is not to establish codes for a "politically correct" sexuality. Politically, feminist activists committed to ending sexual oppression must work to eliminate the oppression of lesbians and gay men as part of an overall movement to enable all women (and men) to freely choose sexual partners.

Feminist activists must take care that our legitimate critiques of heterosexism are not attacks on heterosexual *practice*. As feminists, we must confront those women who do in fact believe that women with heterosexual preferences are either traitors or likely to be anti-lesbian. Condemnation of heterosexual practice has led women who desire sexual relationships with men to feel they cannot participate in feminist movement. They have gotten the message that to be "truly" feminist is not to be heterosexual. It is easy to confuse support for non-oppressive heterosexual practice with the belief in heterosexism. For example, responding to a statement in *Ain't I a Woman* that said, "Attacking heterosexuality does little to strengthen the self-concept of the masses of women who desire to be with men," lesbian feminist Cheryl Clarke writes in her essay "The Failure to Transform: Homophobia in the Black Community":

> Hooks delivers a backhanded slap at lesbian feminists, a considerable number of whom are black. Hooks would have done well to attack the institution of heterosexuality, as it is a prime cause of black women's oppression in America.

Clearly Clarke misunderstands and misinterprets my point. I made no reference to heterosexism, and it is the equation of heterosexual practice with heterosexism that makes it appear that Clarke is attacking the practice itself and not only heterosexism. My point is that feminism will never appeal to a mass-based group of women in our society who are heterosexual if they think that they will be looked down upon or seen as doing something wrong. My comment was not intended to reflect in any way on lesbians, because they are not the only group of feminists that criticizes and in some cases condemns all heterosexual practice.

Just as feminist movement to end sexual oppression should create a social climate in which lesbians and gay men are no longer oppressed, a climate in which their sexual choices are affirmed, it should also create a climate in which heterosexual practice is freed from the constraints of heterosexism and can also be affirmed. One of the practical reasons for doing this is the recognition that the advancement of feminism as a political movement depends on the involvement of masses of women, a vast majority of whom are heterosexual. As long as feminist women (be they celibate, lesbian, heterosexual, etc.) condemn male sexuality, and by extension women who are involved sexually with men, feminist movement is undermined. Useless and unnecessary divisions are created. Concurrently, as long as any pro-heterosexuality statement is read as a hidden attack upon homosexuality, we continue to perpetuate the idea that these are, and should be, competing sexualities. It is possible to delineate the positive or negative aspects of lesbianism without referring in any way to heterosexuality, and vice versa. Although Ellen Willis does not in her essay discuss the notion that lesbianism is a more politically correct sexual choice for feminist women, or that this represents yet another attempt to impose on women a sexual standard, her comments about neo-Victorian logic apply to attacks on female sexual contact with men:

> Neo-Victorians have also undermined feminist opposition to the right, by equating feminism with their own sexual attitudes, in effect reading out of the movement any woman who disagrees with

them. Since their notion of proper feminist sexuality echoes con-
ventional moral judgments and the anti-sexual propaganda pres-
ently coming from the right their guilt-mongering has been quite
effective. Many feminists who are aware that their sexual feelings
contradict the neo-Victorian ideal have lapsed into confused and
apologetic silence. No doubt there are also thousands of women
who have quietly concluded that if this ideal is feminism, then
feminism has nothing to do with them. The result is widespread
apathy, dishonesty, and profound disunity in a movement faced
with a determined enemy that is threatening its very existence.

A feminist movement that aims to eliminate sexist oppression,
and in that context sexual oppression, cannot ignore or dismiss the
choice women make to be heterosexual. Despite heterosexism,
many women have acknowledged and accepted that they do not
have to be heterosexual (that there are other options) and have chosen to be exclusively or primarily heterosexual. Their choices should
be respected. By choosing they exercise sexual freedom. Their
choices may not, as those who oppose them suggest, be influenced
by heterosexual privilege. Most heterosexual privilege is diminished
when compared to the degree of exploitation and oppression a
woman is likely to encounter in most heterosexual relationships.
There are exceptions. Many women choose to be heterosexual because they enjoy genital contact with individual men. Feminist
movement has enriched and added new dimensions to lesbian sexuality, and there is no reason it cannot do the same for heterosexuality. Women with heterosexual preferences need to know that
feminism is a political movement that does not negate their choices
even as it offers a framework to challenge and oppose male sexual
exploitation of women.

There are some feminists (and I am one) who believe that feminist movement to end sexual oppression will not change destructive
sexual norms if individuals are taught that they must choose between competing sexualities (the most obvious being heterosexuality and homosexuality) and conform to the expectations of the
chosen norm. Sexual desire has varied and multiple dimensions and
is rarely as "exclusive" as any norm would suggest. A liberatory sex-

uality would not teach women to see their bodies as accessible to all men, or to all women, for that matter. It would favor instead a sexuality that is open or closed based on the nature of individual interaction. Implicit in the idea of sexual preference is the assumption that anyone of the preferred sex can seek access to one's body. This is a concept that promotes objectification. In a heterosexual context it makes everyone, especially women, into sex objects. Given the power differential created by sexist politics, women are likely to be approached by any man since all men are taught to assume they should have access to the bodies of all women. Sexuality would be transformed if the codes and labels that strip sexual desire of its specificity and particularity were abandoned. As Stephen Heath summarized in *The Sexual Fix:*

> The end of oppression is a recasting of social relations that leaves men and women free, outside of any commodification of the sexual, removed from any of the violence and alienation of circulation and exchange as a sexual identity, the identity of a sex, being fixed to this or that image, this or that norm, to this thing "sexuality."

Though labeled "heterosexual," many women in this society feel little sexual desire for men because of the politics of sexual oppression; male domination destroys and perverts that desire. It is the enormity of acts of sexual oppression imposed on women by men that has made it difficult for women to speak of positive sexual interactions with men. Increasingly, feminist women who are heterosexual are making the point that they choose to have a relationship with an individual man and resist the heterosexist notion that they welcome or are open to the sexual advances of any male. This action attacks the compulsory heterosexuality that denies women the right to choose male sexual partners by evaluating whether such interactions support and affirm them. Asserting their right to choose, women challenge the assumption that female sexuality exists to serve the sexual needs of men. Their efforts enhance the struggle to end sexual oppression. The right to choose must characterize all sexual interactions between individuals.

Lesbians not often to any man... pure feminist

A shift that will undoubtedly emerge as the struggle to end sexual oppression progresses will be decreased obsession with sexuality. This does not necessarily mean that there will be decreased sexual activity. It means that sexuality will no longer have the importance attributed to it in a society that uses sexuality for the express purposes of maintaining gender inequality, male domination, consumerism, and the sexual frustration and unhappiness that deflect attention away from the need to make social revolution. As Stephen Heath comments:

> The real problem and task is always one of social revolution. Privileging the sexual has nothing necessarily liberating about it at all; indeed, it functions only too easily as an instance by development of and reference to which society guarantees its order outside of any effective process of transformation, produces precisely a containing area and ideology of "revolution" or "liberation."

Feminist efforts to develop a political theory of sexuality must continue if sexist oppression is to be eliminated. Yet we must keep in mind that the struggle to end sexual oppression is only one component of a larger struggle to transform society and establish a new social order.

FEMINIST REVOLUTION
Development Through Struggle

Today hardly anyone speaks of feminist revolution. Thinking that revolution would happen simply and quickly, militant feminist activists felt that the great surges of activity—protest, organizing, and consciousness-raising—that characterized the early contemporary feminist movement were all it would take to establish a new social order. Although feminist radicals have always recognized that society must be transformed if sexist oppression is to be eliminated, feminist successes have been mainly in the area of reforms (this is due primarily to the efforts and visions of radical groups like Bread and Roses and the Combahee River Collective, etc.). Such reforms have helped many women make significant strides towards social equality with men in a number of areas within the present white supremacist, patriarchal system, but these reforms have not corresponded with decreased sexist exploitation and/or oppression. Prevailing sexist values and assumptions remain intact, and it has been easy for politically conservative anti-feminists to undermine feminist reforms. Many politically progressive critics of feminist movement see the impulse towards reforms as counterproductive. Arguing in favor of reforms as a stage in revolutionary process in her essay "Feminism: Reform or Revolution," Sandra Harding writes:

> It could well be that the reformers have in mind a long-range goal, which is something like a picture of a new society. The reforms fill in that picture bit by bit. Some pieces can be filled in with

comparatively little trouble (e.g., equal pay for equal work), other
pieces are filled in only with great difficulty (e.g., equal access
to every job). But whether the difficulty is great or small, there is
always a precedent in the society—somewhere—for each kind
of change, and the only changes demanded are those which fill in
the picture of the desired new society. Thus at the end of a long
series of small quantitative changes, everything would have
changed gradually so that the whole system was completely different.... On this alternative model a series of reforms might constitute a revolution.

Reforms can be a vital part of the movement towards revolution,
but what is important are the types of reforms that are initiated.
Feminist focus on reforms to improve the social status of women
within the existing social structure allowed women and men to lose
sight of the need for total transformation of society. The Equal
Rights Amendment (ERA) campaign, for example, diverted a great
deal of money and human resources towards a reform effort that
should have been a massive political campaign to build a feminist
constituency. This constituency would have guaranteed the success
of the ERA. Unfortunately, revolutionary reforms focused first and
foremost on educating masses of women and men about feminist
movement, showing them ways it would transform their lives for
the better, were not initiated. Instead, women involved with feminist reforms were inclined to think less about transforming society
and more about fighting for equality and equal rights with men.

Many radical activists in the women's movement who were not
interested in obtaining social equality with men in the existing social
structure chose to attack exploitative and oppressive sexist behavior. Identifying men as the villains, the "enemy," they concentrated
their attention on exposing male "evil." One example of this has
been the critique and attack on pornography. It is obvious that pornography promotes degradation of women, sexism, and sexualized
violence. It is also obvious that endless denunciations of pornography are fruitless if there is not greater emphasis on transforming society and, by implication, sexuality. This more significant struggle
has not been seriously attended to by feminist movement. (A fuller

discussion of the politics of feminist anti-pornography effort may be found in Alice Echols's essay "Cultural Feminism: Feminist Capitalism and the Anti-Pornography Movement.") The focus on "men" and "male behavior" has overshadowed emphasis on women developing themselves politically so that we can begin making the cultural transformations that would pave the way for the establishment of a new social order. Much feminist consciousness-raising has centered on helping women to understand the nature of sexism in personal life, especially as it relates to male dominance. While this is a necessary task, it is not the only task for consciousness-raising.

Feminist consciousness-raising has not significantly pushed women in the direction of revolutionary politics. For the most part, it has not helped women understand capitalism—how it works as a system that exploits female labor and its interconnections with sexist oppression. It has not urged women to learn about different political systems like socialism or encouraged women to invent and envision new political systems. It has not attacked materialism and our society's addiction to overconsumption. It has not shown women how we benefit from the exploitation and oppression of women and men globally or shown us ways to oppose imperialism. Most importantly, is has not continually confronted women with the understanding that feminist movement to end sexist oppression can be successful only if we are committed to revolution, to the establishment of a new social order.

New social orders are established gradually. This is hard for individuals in the United States to accept. We have either been socialized to believe that revolutions are always characterized by extreme violence between the oppressed and their oppressors or that revolutions happen quickly. We have also been taught to crave immediate gratification of our desires and swift responses to our demands. Like every other liberation movement in this society, feminism has suffered because these attitudes keep participants from forming the kind of commitment to protracted struggle that makes revolution possible. As a consequence, feminist movement has not sustained its revolutionary momentum. It has been a successful rebellion. Differentiating between rebellion and revolution, Grace Lee Boggs and James Boggs emphasize:

> Rebellion is a stage in the development of revolution, but it is not revolution. It is an important stage because it represents the "standing up," the assertion of their humanity on the part of the oppressed. Rebellion informs both the oppressed and everybody else that a situation has become intolerable. They establish a form of communication among the oppressed themselves and at the same time open the eyes and ears of people who have been blind and deaf to the fate of their fellow citizens. Rebellions break the threads that have been holding the system together and throw into question the legitimacy and the supposed permanence of existing institutions. They shake up old values so that relations between individuals and between groups within the society are unlikely ever to be the same again. The inertia of the society has been interrupted. Only by understanding what a rebellion accomplishes can we see its limitations. A rebellion disrupts the society, but it does not provide what is necessary to establish a new social order.

Although feminist rebellion has been a success, it is not leading to further revolutionary development. Internally its progress is retarded by those feminist activists who do not feel that the movement exists for the advancement of all women and men, who seem to think it exists to advance individual participants, who are threatened by opinions and ideas that differ from the dominant feminist ideology, who seek to suppress and silence dissenting voices, who do not acknowledge the necessity for continued effort to create a liberatory ideology. These women resist efforts to critically examine prevailing feminist ideology and refuse to acknowledge its limitations. Externally the progress of feminist movement is retarded by organized anti-feminist activity and by the political indifference of masses of women and men who are not well-enough acquainted with either side of the issue to take a stand.

To move beyond the stage of feminist rebellion, to move past the impasse that characterizes contemporary feminist movement, women must recognize the need for reorganization. Without dismissing the positive dimensions of feminist movement up to this point, we need to accept that there was never a strategy on the part of feminist organizers and participants to build mass awareness of the need for feminist movement through political education. Such a strategy is needed if feminism is to be a political movement impacting on society as a whole in a revolutionary and transformative way. We also need to face the fact that many of the dilemmas facing feminist movement today were created by bourgeois women who shaped the movement in ways that served their opportunistic class interests. We must now work to change its direction so that women of all classes can see that their interest in ending sexist oppression is served by feminist movement. Recognizing that bourgeois opportunists have exploited feminist movement should not be seen as an attack upon all bourgeois women. There are individual bourgeois women who are repudiating class privilege; who are politically progressive; who have given, are giving, or are willing to give of themselves in a revolutionary way to advance feminist movement. Reshaping the class politics of feminist movement is strategy that will lead women from all classes to join feminist struggle.

To build a mass-based feminist movement, we need to have a liberatory ideology that can be shared with everyone. That revolutionary ideology can be created only if the experiences of people on the margin who suffer sexist oppression and other forms of group oppression are understood, addressed, and incorporated. They must participate in feminist movement as makers of theory and as leaders of action. In past feminist practice, we have been satisfied with relying on self-appointed individuals, some of whom are more concerned about exercising authority and power than with communicating with people from various backgrounds and political perspectives. Such individuals do not choose to learn about collective female experience, but impose their own ideas and values. Leaders are needed, and should be individuals who acknowledge their relationship to the group and who are accountable to it. They should have the ability to show love and compassion, show this love through their actions, and be able to engage in successful dialogue. Such love, Paulo Freire suggests, acts to transform domination:

Dialogue cannot exist, however, in the absence of profound love for the world and for women and men. The naming of the world, which is an act of creation and re-creation, is not possible if it is not infused with love. Love is at the same time the foundation of dialogue and dialogue itself. It is thus necessarily the task of responsible subjects and cannot exist in a relation of domination. Domination reveals the pathology of love: sadism in the dominator and masochism in the dominated. Because love is an act of courage, not of fear, love is commitment to others. No matter where the oppressed are found, the act of love is commitment to their cause—the cause of liberation. And this commitment, because it is loving, is dialogical.

Women must begin the work of feminist reorganization with the understanding that we have all (irrespective of our race, sex, or class) acted in complicity with the existing oppressive system. We all need to make a conscious break with the system. Some of us make this break sooner than others. The compassion we extend to ourselves, the recognition that our change in consciousness and action has been a process, must characterize our approach to those individuals who are politically unconscious. We cannot motivate them to join feminist struggle by asserting a political superiority that makes the movement just another oppressive hierarchy.

Before we can address the masses, we must recapture the attention, the support, the participation of the many women who were once active in feminist movement and who left disillusioned. Too many women have abandoned feminist movement because they cannot support the ideas of a small minority of women who have hegemonic control over feminist discourse—the development of the theory that informs practice. Too many women who have caring bonds with men have drifted away from feminist movement because they feel that identification of "man as enemy" is an unconstructive paradigm. Too many women have ceased to support feminist struggle because the ideology has been too dogmatic, too absolutist, too closed. Too many women have left feminist movement because they were identified as the "enemy." Feminist activists would do well to heed the words of Susan Griffin when she reminds us in her essay "The Way of All Ideology":

> A deeply political knowledge of the world does not lead to a creation of an enemy. Indeed, to create monsters unexplained by circumstance is to forget the political vision which above all explains behavior as emanating from circumstance, a vision which believes in a capacity born to all human beings for creation, joys, and kindness, in a human nature which, under the right circumstances, can bloom.
>
> When a movement for liberation inspires itself chiefly by a hatred for an enemy rather than from this vision of possibility, it begins to defeat itself. Its very notions cease to be healing. Despite the fact that it declares itself in favor of liberation, its language is no longer liberatory. It begins to require a censorship within itself. Its ideas of truth become more and more narrow. And the movement that began with a moving evocation of truth begins to appear fraudulent from the outside, begins to mirror all that it says it opposes, for now it, too, is an oppressor of certain truths, and speakers, and begins, like the old oppressors, to hide from itself.

To restore the revolutionary life force to feminist movement, women and men must begin to rethink and reshape its direction. While we must recognize, acknowledge, and appreciate the significance of feminist rebellion and the women (and men) who made it happen, we must be willing to criticize, re-examine, and begin feminist work anew, a challenging task because we lack historical precedents. There are many ways to make revolution. Revolutions can be and usually are initiated by violent overthrow of an existing political structure. In the United States, women and men committed to feminist struggle know that we are far outpowered by our opponents, that they not only have access to every type of weaponry known to humankind, but they have both the learned consciousness to do and accept violence as well as the skill to perpetuate it. Therefore, this cannot be the basis for feminist revolution in this society. Our emphasis must be on cultural transformation: destroying dualism, eradicating systems of domination. Our struggle will be gradual and protracted. Any effort to make feminist revolution here can be aided by the example of liberation struggles led by oppressed peoples globally who resist formidable powers.

The formation of an oppositional world view is necessary for feminist struggle. This means that the world we have most intimately known, the world in which we feel "safe" (even if such feelings are based on illusions), must be radically changed. Perhaps it is the knowledge that everyone must change, not just those we label enemies or oppressors, that has so far served to check our revolutionary impulses. Those revolutionary impulses must freely inform our theory and practice if feminist movement to end existing oppression is to progress, if we are to transform our present reality.

BIBLIOGRAPHY

Amos, Valerie, and Pratibha Parmar. "Challenging Imperial Feminism," *Feminist Review,* Autumn 1984.

André, Rae. *Homemakers: The Forgotten Workers.* Chicago: University of Chicago Press, 1981.

Angelou, Maya. "Interview," in *Black Women Writers at Work.* Ed. Claudia Tate. New York: Continuum Publishing, 1983.

Aptheker, Bettina. *Woman's Legacy: Essays on Race, Sex, and Class in American History.* Amherst: University of Massachusetts Press, 1982.

Babcox, Deborah, and Madeline Bekin, eds. *Liberation Now! Writings from the Women's Liberation Movement.* New York: Dell, 1971.

Badinter, Elisabeth. *Mother Love.* New York: Macmillan, 1981.

Barber, Benjamin. *Liberating Feminism.* New York: Dell, 1975.

Berg, Barbara. *The Remembered Gate: Origins of American Feminism.* New York: Oxford University Press, 1979.

Bernard, Jessie. *The Future of Motherhood.* New York: Dial, 1974.

Bird, Caroline. *The Two-Paycheck Marriage.* New York: Rocket Books, 1979.

Boggs, Grace Lee, and James Boggs. *Revolution and Evolution in the Twentieth Century.* New York: Monthly Review Press, 1974.

Brown, Rita Mae. "The Last Straw," in *Class and Feminism.* Eds. Charlotte Bunch and Nancy Myron. Baltimore: Diana Press, 1974, pp. 14–23.

Bunch, Charlotte. "Feminism and Education: Not by Degrees." *Quest,* Vol. V, No. 1 (Summer 1979), pp. 1–7.

Bunch, Charlotte, and Nancy Myron, eds. *Class and Feminism: A Collection of Essays from the Furies.* Baltimore: Diana Press, 1974.

Cagan, Leslie. "Talking Disarmament," *South End Press News,* Vol. 2, No. 2 (Spring/Summer 1983), pp. 1–7.

Cartledge, Sue, and Joanna Ryan, eds. *Sex and Love: New Thoughts on Old Con-*

traditions. London: Women's Press, 1983.

Cassell, Joan. *A Group Called Women: Sisterhood and Symbolism in the Feminist Movement*. New York: McKay, 1977.

Chesler, Phyllis. *With Child: A Diary of Motherhood*. New York: Crowell, 1979.

Chesler, Phyllis, and Emily Jane Goodman. *Women, Money, and Power*. New York: William Morrow and Company, 1976.

Chodorow, Nancy. *The Reproduction of Mothering: Psychoanalysis and the Sociology of Gender*. Berkeley: University of California Press, 1978.

Clarke, Cheryl. "The Failure to Transform: Homophobia in the Black Community," in *Home Girls: A Black Feminist Anthology*. Ed. Barbara Smith. New York: Kitchen Table: Women of Color Press, 1983, pp. 197–208.

Coles, Robert, and Jane Coles. *Women of Crisis*. New York: Dell Publishing Company, 1978.

Cornwell, Anita. "Three for the Price of One: Notes from a Gay Black Feminist," in *Lavender Culture*. Eds. Karla Jay and Allen Young. New York: Jove Books (Harcourt Brace Jovanovich), 1978, pp. 466–76.

Coward, Rosalind. *Female Desire*. London: Paladin, 1984.

Daly, Mary. *Beyond God the Father: Toward a Philosophy of Women's Liberation*. Boston: Beacon Press, 1973.

Delphy, Christine. *Close to Home: A Materialist Analysis of Women's Oppression*. Trans. Diana Leonard. Amherst: University of Massachusetts Press, 1984.

——. "For a Materialist Feminism," trans. Elaine Marks, in *New French Feminisms*. Eds. Elaine Marks and Isabelle De Courtivron. Amherst: University of Massachusetts Press, 1980, pp. 197–98.

Dixon, Marlene. *Women in Class Struggle*. San Francisco: Synthesis Publications, 1980.

Echols, Alice. "Cultural Feminism: Feminist Capitalism and the Anti-Pornography Movement," *Social Text* (Spring/Summer 1983), pp. 34–57.

Ehrenreich, Barbara, and Karin Stallard. "The Nouveau Poor," *Ms.*, August 1983, pp. 217–24.

Ehrlich, Carol. "The Unhappy Marriage of Marxism and Feminism: Can It Be Saved?," in *Women and Revolution*. Ed. Lydia Sargent. Boston: South End Press, 1981, pp. 109–33.

Eisenstein, Zillah. *The Radical Future of Liberal Feminism*. New York: Longman, 1981.

Enloe, Cynthia. *Does Khaki Become You?: The Militarization of Women's Lives*.

Boston: South End Press, 1983.

Evans, Sara. *Personal Politics: The Roots of Women's Liberation in the Civil Rights Movement and the New Left.* New York: Knopf, 1979.

Fanon, Frantz. *Black Skin, White Masks.* New York: Grove Press, 1967.

Fouque, Antoinette. "Warnings," in *New French Feminisms.* Eds. Elaine Marks and Isabelle De Courtivron. Amherst: University of Massachusetts Press, 1980, pp. 117–18.

Freeman, Jo. *The Politics of Women's Liberation.* New York: David McKay Company, 1975.

Freire, Paulo. *Pedagogy of the Oppressed.* New York: Seabury, 1970.

Friday, Nancy. *My Mother/My Self: The Daughter's Search for Identity.* New York: Delacorte, 1977.

Friedan, Betty. *The Feminine Mystique.* New York: W. W. Norton Company, 1963.

Fritz, Leah. *Dreamers and Dealers: An Intimate Appraisal of the Women's Movement.* Boston: Beacon Press, 1979.

Goodman, Ellen. "The Turmoil of Teenage Sexuality," *Ms.*, Vol. XII, No. 1 (July 1983), pp. 37–41.

Goodman, Gerre, et al. *No Turning Back: Lesbian and Gay Liberation of the '80s.* Philadelphia: New Society Press, 1983.

Gornick, Vivian. *Essays in Feminism.* New York: Harper and Row, 1978.

Greene, Bob. "Sisters—Under the Skin," *San Francisco Examiner,* May 15, 1983.

Greer, Germaine. *The Female Eunuch.* New York: McGraw-Hill, 1971.

——. *Sex and Destiny: The Politics of Human Fertility.* New York: Harper and Row, 1984.

Griffin, Susan. "The Way of All Ideology," *Signs,* Spring 1982.

Gross, Jeanne. "Feminist Ethics from a Marxist Perspective," *Radical Religion,* Vol. III, No. 2 (1977), pp. 52–56.

Hanisch, Carol. "Men's Liberation," in *Feminist Revolution,* Redstockings, 1975, pp. 60–63.

Harding, Sandra. "Feminism: Reform or Revolution," in *Women and Philosophy.* Eds. Carol Gould and Marx Wartofsky. New York: G. P. Putnam, 1976, pp. 271–84.

Hartsock, Nancy. "Political Change: Two Perspectives on Power," in *Building Feminist Theory: Essays from Quest.* New York: Longman, 1981, pp. 3–19.

Heath, Stephen. *The Sexual Fix.* London: Macmillan, 1982.

Hellman, Lillian. *Pentimento.* Boston: Little, Brown, 1973.

Hodge, John. *The Cultural Basis of Racism and Group Oppression.* Berkeley: Time Readers Press, 1975.

Hornacek, Paul. "Anti-Sexist Consciousness-Raising Groups for Men," in *For Men Against Sexism: A Book of Readings.* Ed. John Snodgrass. Albion: Times Change Press, 1977.

Janeway, Elizabeth. *Cross Sections.* New York: William Morrow, 1982.

——. *Powers of the Weak.* New York: Morrow Quill, 1981.

Joseph, Gloria. "The Incompatible Ménage à Trois: Marxism, Feminism, and Racism," in *Women and Revolution.* Ed. Lydia Sargent. Boston: South End Press, 1981.

Kennedy, Florynce. "Institutionalized Oppression vs. The Female," in *Sisterhood Is Powerful.* Ed. Robin Morgan. New York: Vintage Books, 1970, pp. 438–46.

Koedt, Anne, Ellen Levine, and Anita Rapore, eds., *Radical Feminism.* New York: Quadrangle Books, 1973.

Koen, Susan, Nina Swain, and Friends, eds. *Ain't Nowhere We Can Run: A Handbook for Women on the Nuclear Mentality.* Norwich, VT: WAND, 1980, p. 2.

Kollias, Karen. "Class Realities: Create a New Power Base," *Quest,* Vol. I, No. 3 (Winter 1975), pp. 28–43.

Leon, Barbara. "Separate to Integrate," in *Feminist Revolution.* Redstockings, 1975, pp. 139–44.

Malos, Ellen, ed. *The Politics of Housework.* New York: Allison and Busby, 1982.

Markovic, Mihailo. "Women's Liberation and Human Emancipation," in *Women and Philosophy.* Eds. Carol Gould and Marx Wartofsky. New York: G. P. Putnam, 1976, pp. 145–67.

McCandless, Cathy. "Some Thoughts about Racism, Classism, and Separatism," in *Top Ranking.* Eds. Joan Gibbs and Sara Bennett. New York: February Third Press, 1979, pp. 105–15.

Montgomery, Helen. *Western Women in Eastern Lands.* New York: Macmillan, 1910.

Moraga, Cherríe. *Loving in the War Years: lo que nunca pasó por sus labios.* Boston: South End Press, 1983.

Morgan, Robin, ed. *Sisterhood Is Powerful: An Anthology of Writings from the Women's Liberation Movement.* New York: Random House, 1970.

Morrison, Toni. "Cinderella's Stepsisters," *Ms.,* September 1979, pp. 41–42.

——. "What the Black Woman Thinks about Women's Lib," *The New York*

Times Magazine, August 22, 1971.

Oakley, Ann. *The Sociology of Housework.* New York: Pantheon, 1975.

Patrick, Jane. "A Special Report on Love, Violence, and the Single Woman," *Mademoiselle,* October 1982, pp. 188, 189, 240, 242.

Person, Ethel Spector. "Sexuality as the Mainstay of Identity: Psychoanalytic Perspectives," in *Women: Sex and Sexuality.* Eds. Catherine Stimpson and Ethel Spector Person. Chicago: University of Chicago Press, 1980, pp. 36–61.

"Redstockings Manifesto," in *Sisterhood Is Powerful: An Anthology of Writings from the Women's Liberation Movement.* Ed. Robin Morgan. New York: Random House, 1970, pp. 533–36.

Rich, Adrienne. *Of Woman Born.* New York: W. W. Norton, 1976.

Ruddick, Sara. "Maternal Thinking," in *Rethinking the Family: Some Feminist Questions.* Ed. Barrie Thorne with Marilyn Yalom. New York: Longman, 1982, pp. 76–93.

Rule, Jane. "With All Due Respect," in *Outlander.* Tallahassee, FL: Naiad Press, 1981.

Saffioti, Heleieth I.B. *Women in Class Society.* Trans. Michael Vale. New York: Monthly Review Press, 1978.

Schechter, Susan. *Women and Male Violence: The Visions and Struggles of the Battered Women's Movement.* Boston: South End Press, 1982.

Schoonmaker, Mary Ellen. "Bringing Up Baby," *In These Times,* September 7, 1983, pp. 12, 13, 22.

Smith, Barbara. "Notes for Yet Another Paper on Black Feminism, Or, Will the Real Enemy Please Stand Up?," *Conditions: Five,* Vol. 11, No. 2 (Autumn 1979), pp. 123–27.

——, ed. *Home Girls: A Black Feminist Anthology.* New York: Kitchen Table: Women of Color Press, 1983.

Snitow, Ann, Christine Stansell, and Sharon Thompson, eds. *Powers of Desire: The Politics of Sexuality.* New York: Monthly Review Press, 1983.

Snodgrass, Jon, ed. *For Men Against Sexism: A Book of Readings.* Albion: Times Change Press, 1977.

Spelman, Elizabeth. "Theories of Race and Gender/The Erasure of Black Women," *Quest,* Vol. V, No. 4 (1982), pp. 36–62.

Stambler, Sookie, comp. *Women's Liberation: Blueprint for the Future.* New York: Ace Books, 1970.

Thorne, Barrie. "Feminist Rethinking of the Family: An Overview," in *Rethinking the Family: Some Feminist Questions.* Ed. Barrie Thorne with Marilyn Yalom. New York: Longman, 1982.

Valeska, Lucia. "If All Else Fails, I'm Still a Mother." *Quest,* Vol. I, No. 3 (Winter 1975).

Vazquez, Carmen. "Towards a Revolutionary Ethics," *Coming Up,* January 1983, p. 11.

Walton, Patty. "The Culture in Our Blood," *Women: A Journal of Liberation,* Vol. VIII, No. 1 (January 1982), pp. 43–45.

Ware, Cellestine. *Woman Power: The Movement for Women's Liberation.* New York: Tower Publications, 1970.

Willis, Ellen. "Toward a Feminist Sexual Revolution," *Social Text* (Fall 1982), pp. 3–21.

Women and the New World. Detroit: Advocators, 1976.

INDEX

About the Author

bell hooks is the author of numerous critically acclaimed and influential books on the politics of race, gender, class, and culture. Her first book, *Ain't I a Woman: Black Women and Feminism* (South End Press, 1981), was named one of the "twenty most influential women's books of the last twenty years" by *Publishers Weekly* in 1992. She has published several other books with South End Press, including *Sisters of the Yam, Black Looks, Yearning, Talking Back,* and *Breaking Bread* (with Cornel West). A frequent lecturer in the United States and abroad, she is Distinguished Professor of English at City College, City University of New York. Her most recent book from South End Press is *Feminism Is for Everybody: Passionate Politics.*

About South End Press

South End Press is a nonprofit, collectively run book publisher with more than 200 titles in print. Since our founding in 1977, we have tried to meet the needs of readers who are exploring, or are already committed to, the politics of radical social change. Our goal is to publish books that encourage critical thinking and constructive action on the key political, cultural, social, economic, and ecological issues shaping life in the United States and in the world. In this way, we hope to give expression to a wide diversity of democratic social movements and to provide an alternative to the products of corporate publishing.

Through the Institute for Social and Cultural Change, South End Press works with other political media projects—Z magazine; Speakout, a speakers' bureau; and Alternative Radio—to expand access to information and critical analysis.

To order books, please send a check or money order to: South End Press, 7 Brookline Street, #1, Cambridge, MA 02139-4146. To order by credit card, call 1-800-533-8478. Please include $3.50 for postage and handling for the first book and 50 cents for each additional book. Write for a free catalog, or visit our web site, http://www.southendpress.org.

Other South End Press Titles by bell hooks

Ain't I a Woman: Black Women and Feminism	$15
Black Looks: Race and Representation	$15
Breaking Bread: Insurgent Black Intellectual Life (with Cornel West)	$16
Feminism Is for Everybody: Passionate Politics	$12
Sisters of the Yam: Black Women and Self-Recovery	$15
Talking Back: Thinking Feminist, Thinking Black	$15
Yearning: Race, Gender, and Cultural Politics	$17

Other South End Press Classics
Series Editor: Manning Marable

Strike! by Jeremy Brecher	$22
Detroit: I Do Mind Dying (A Study in Urban Revolution) by Dan Georgakas and Marvin Surkin	$18
Fateful Triangle: The United States, Israel, and the Palestinians by Noam Chomsky	$22
How Capitalism Underdeveloped Black America by Manning Marable	$22
Loving in the War Years Cherríe L. Moraga	$17